Psychic Protection

BEGINNINGS:
A DRAGONHAWK SERIES

Psychic Protection

Ted Andrews

DRAGONHAWK PUBLISHING   JACKSON, TENNESSEE

A DRAGONHAWK PUBLISHING BOOK

First Edition
Second Printing

Cover design by Ted Andrews

Editing and indexing by
Pagyn Alexander-Harding (IAAI, Hitterdal, MN)

Book layout, text design, and vintage etchings provided by
Diane Haugen (Whiskey Creek Document Design, Barnesville, MN)

ISBN 1-888767-30-8

Library of Congress Catalog Card Number: 98-84419

This book was designed and produced by

Dragonhawk Publishing
Jackson, Tennessee
USA

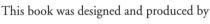

Dedication

To Akasha, with love

OTHER TITLES BY TED ANDREWS

DRAGONHAWK PUBLISHING TITLES
Treasures of the Unicorn
Music Therapy for Non-Musicians (BEGINNINGS Series)
More Simplified Magic

MUSIC AND SPOKEN AUDIO THROUGH LIFE MAGIC ENTERPRISES
Roses of Light
Upon the Wings of Angels
Mystery of the Fire Spirits
Uncover Your Past Lives
Psychic Protection
Discover Your Spirit Animal
Entering the Tree of Life

BOOKS BY TED ANDREWS THROUGH LLEWELLYN PUBLICATIONS
Simplified Magic
Imagick
Sacred Power in Your Name
How to See and Read the Aura
The Magical Name
Dream Alchemy
How to Uncover Your Past Lives
Sacred Sounds
How to Meet and Work with Spirit Guides
How to Heal with Color
Magickal Dance
Enchantment of the Faerie Realm
The Occult Christ: Angelic Mysteries & the Divine Feminine
Animal-Speak
The Healer's Manual
How to Develop and Use Psychic Touch
Crystal Balls & Crystal Bowls

BEGINNINGS

Every day more and more people begin to explore the mystical realms of life. While some find their searches rewarded, too often the seekers find themselves lost, discouraged, frustrated, and overwhelmed. Because of this, Dragonhawk Publishing has established BEGINNINGS, a series of books to guide the true seeker safely into the realms of wonder, mystery, and human possibility.

Whether seeking psychic power, effective healing tools and techniques, a closer connection with Nature, or a greater realization of your own inner potentials and creativity, there are two important keys. The *first key* is realizing that this is not just for the few and gifted. Everyone has the ability to develop that potential.

The *second key* is having the right teacher. To this end, Dragonhawk Publishing has enlisted internationally recognized author, storyteller, and mystic Ted Andrews to shepherd this series. One of the most dynamic teachers and leaders in the field today, he touches thousands upon thousands every year through his books and his seminars.

All journeys begin with the first step. Whether truly a beginner or one who has walked the path, our BEGINNINGS series will help you experience and renew the wonders of yourself and of life. You will safely explore new realms and new possibilities. And you will realize a truth that all seekers eventually uncover:

We are never given a hope, wish, or dream
without also being given opportunities
to make them a reality!

Ted Andrews

TABLE OF CONTENTS

Part I: Removing the Veils

Part II: Becoming the Spiritual Warrior

Part III: Walking the Spiritual Path

ILLUSTRATIONS

TABLES

EXERCISES

 * These three exercises are available in audio tape.
See pp. 356-357.

TOOLS

Introduction

Why Psychic Self-Defense?

THE FORTUNE TELLER[1]

Long ago and not so long ago, a young man was discouraged with life. It seemed that all he ever did was work, and yet he dreamed of so much more—adventure, wealth and, of course, romance. Surely there had to be more to life than struggling every day.

One day he heard of a festival in a distant village, and it excited him more than usual. At other festivals he had attended as a child he had witnessed performers, song and dance. He had even seen the occasional fortune teller. Although he was not truly a believer in such, he felt that if he were to do something more with his life, it would be better to know now than to live on false hope. He decided to visit the

---

[1] The origins of many folk tales and fables are often fogged—variations are found within many societies and traditions. This version is a variation of an old West African tale.

festival in the hopes of finding a fortune teller, one who would be able to predict his future.

It was many hours of walking to the festival, and he arrived at dusk. The town was alive with music and dancing and people selling their wares. Though he had journeyed most of the day, his heart pounded with the excitement and color of the festival. He wandered the streets and booths, looking and drinking in the festivities, his eyes searching for the sign of any mystic or fortune teller.

On the very outskirts of town, at the edge of the festivities, he spied a small tent with a sign out front: FORTUNES TOLD. The young man's heart jumped, and he moved to the open flap. He took a deep breath and peered inside. An old man was seated at a rickety old table, whose legs were as thin and wobbly as his own. The boy's body cast a shadow into the room, and the old man looked up.

"Come to have your fortune told?"

The old man's voice was strong and confident, and the boy just nodded. The old man stood and gestured to a chair across from him. The boy eyed the chair and moved eagerly to sit down. Before he could, the old man reached out and took a gentle but strong hold of the young man's shoulder.

"But first there is the matter of my fee...."

The young man's eyes narrowed, questioning—a bit distrustful. Before he could respond though the old fortune teller continued.

"After all, that shouldn't be a problem for one who will surely encounter great wealth some day."

The young man's heart jumped.

"You mean I truly will be rich!"

The old man said nothing, keeping his own expression blank. When nothing else was forthcoming, the boy quickly fumbled in his pocket and dropped a handful of silver coins upon the table. The old man scooped them up and out of sight, and his expressionless face smiled at the young man. He gestured for the boy to sit, and nodded his head vigorously.

"Oh, most certainly," he told the young man, "As long as you find the right job and save your money."

The young man breathed a sigh of wonder and excitement, already envisioning what he would do with all of his future wealth. As the young man sat down, the fortune teller asked, "What else would you like to know?"

"Will I be famous as well as rich?" the young man asked earnestly.

The fortune teller paused, as if waiting communication from the divine, and then closed his eyes. He answered solemnly.

"I most definitely see you as being famous," he replied. "Especially once you become well known."

The young man beamed and leaned forward, anxious to hear even more of his future.

"Will I be married...happily?"

Again the fortune teller paused, his eyes closed as if drawing his answers from some mysterious spiritual source.

"You will marry," the old fortune teller proclaimed. "And she will be your true love once you find her and she accepts.

Ted Andrews

The two of you will be as happy as any have ever been in the world if together you avoid misery."

The young man was ecstatic. He always believed there was more in store for him, but never had he hoped there would be so much.

"And will I have a long life?" The young man held his breath, afraid that with so much good having been forecast that surely it would all be cut short.

"Hmm." The old fortune teller seemed lost for a moment. Then he nodded as if to some invisible spirit. "Yes, I see," he spoke to the air above him as if speaking to an invisible spirit. Then the old man opened his eyes and looked into the wide eyes of the young man.

"You shall have a very long life," he said after a tense pause. "As long as you stay healthy. Then only an early demise could possibly shorten it."

The young man leaped from his chair, his face beaming with joy. He grabbed the hand of the old fortune teller and pumped it vigorously. And when words of gratitude failed him, he embraced the old man and then dashed from the tent. He was positive his good fortune would begin for him on his journey home.

We are living in a time of great change and contradiction. Technologically, our society has achieved more than even imagined 50 years ago, and yet the rise in mysticism and things less scientifically substantial has also exceeded what anyone imagined. Medical breakthroughs are occurring every day, and yet more and more people are turning to holistic modalities.

The number of churches and branches of religions have expanded as in no other time in history, and yet, more and more people are discontent with their churches and are leaving them, looking elsewhere for answers. We live in a time of new materials, new tools, new instruments, and new powers. Yet there is an increasing human participation in old religions, past civilizations, and ancient mysticism.

Today people experiment daily with new and often strange self-help techniques, looking for ways to empower themselves and to take greater control over their lives. Science has taken to studying such things as telepathy, precognitive dreams, psychic phenomena, and other areas previously considered quite irrational and occult.

Boundaries are changing. The medical world accepts the possibility of healing through herbs and other holistic modalities, and quantum physics has silenced much of the scoffing about other dimensions and realms. Much of what used to be considered the stuff of fiction, much of what was once considered metaphysical mumbo-jumbo, is now recognized to have strong threads of truth running through it.

What was once considered quite irrational is now acceptable. What was once considered weird and evil, with no relevance to the modern world, is now being explored from new scientific parameters. We live in a time of information abundance that demands greater personal responsibility, but results in a great deal of dabbling and experimenting.

Amidst this information boom and the technological expansion of modern society, there arose a movement for integrating the ancient mysticism and teachings with modern science and technology. People began to look to the past, since the present was changing so rapidly. People began to seek ways of integrating the psychic with psychology, healing with modern medicine, mysticism with science, the past with the present.

This New Age Movement has now become enmeshed with mainstream life, so much so that it has become big business. Every week in most major cities across the country, psychic fairs are held, drawing hundreds and even thousands of attendees. Bookstores maintain their own New Age or metaphysical sections to cover the multitude of titles that are published on every possible facet, from holistic healing to hauntings, from UFOs to psychic development for the workplace. People are seeking the spiritual. They are seeking answers to the mysteries of life as never before.

As with most things, whenever there arises a tremendous availability of knowledge to the general public in any area of life, false assumptions and their ensuing problems also arise. Two are most common. First, there occurs the assumption that because something is in print, the material is true and beneficial—that the author is a well-founded authority. Second, there arises the assumption that since it is in print, that anyone can use the information safely, easily with no repercussions.

The problem with these two assumptions is that most people don't take the time or never learned how to discern and discriminate in regards to what they are taught, whether through books or any other medium. They fail to ask themselves and others if the teachings are true. Half true? Or completely false? Many do not know how we determine the half-truths from the whole truths.

Whenever we enter a new arena of study and exploration, especially that of the psychic realm— discrimination and discernment are even more necessary. When it is a realm of study whose boundaries and influences are foreign and not always subject to strict scientific verification, discrimination becomes even more essential. It is because of this that most people can benefit from instruction in the art and techniques of psychic protection.

People must learn that the only one who truly knows better for them is themselves. We can use books and other teachers to assist us, but it is up to each of us to take the information and test it, finding its benefit for us within our own life circumstances. Even St. Paul said, "Test all things and hold fast to that which is true."

Although this book provides techniques that will benefit anyone in any field of life, helping to keep them stronger and more balanced, it is primarily for the thousands upon thousands who are working in, studying, or linked in any way to the psychic and metaphysical fields. This includes anyone involved in Wicca, magic, mysticism, psychic development, holistic healing, UFOs, or any area that can be considered a part of the New Age or metaphysical genre. This book will help you to sort through and stay grounded while exploring other possibilities to the mystery of life.

I have been involved in this field and the various aspects of it for most of my life. I have been very seriously studying and developing my personal abilities within it for over thirty years. It has been a full time career for more than fifteen years.

Into this career I brought an extensive formal (both undergraduate and graduate) and informal education, along with ten years of teaching and counseling experience from the public school system. Each year I travel extensively throughout the country teaching and lecturing, making between

75 and 100 appearances, working with thousands of people. In my travels, I see people mislead, manipulated, giving up their own power, and hurt inappropriately. I see workers in this field drained, depressed, and overwrought, struggling physically, emotionally, mentally, spiritually, and financially.

Some who work in this field may take offense at what I say. I do not offer an apology. If this book and some of its statements make you think and examine how and what you do, paying more attention to how you affect others, then it serves a purpose. If this book prevents even one person from being mislead or drained or taken advantage of, then the book has done its job.

This handbook will examine the myths and misconceptions about the psychic world and energy. It is a book of pragmatic spirituality, helping you to understand your energy and potentials and to work with them more safely by honoring yourself and your feelings as you seek and awaken more fully to the world around you.

For those who are not a part of the psychic and metaphysical world, this is still a book of protection that you can use. Whether you are a caretaker of the home, a parent, a business man or woman, healer, psychic, agnostic, or priest, you will find something in this book that will help you, something that you can apply to your own life for greater health and balance.

We are all affected by a myriad of influences, most of which go unnoticed. These include both sound and light frequencies, along with electrical, chemical, and even thought influences that impact upon us daily. Separate and together they can create tremendous stress. As that stress accumulates, we begin to experience and manifest dis-ease and imbalance.

This book is about protection against those subtle influences in life. It is a book of protection of our psyche, our energy, our essence, and our lives. It is a handbook that anyone can use to enhance their lives and feel more balanced and in control by helping you to understand how easily influenced you can be on a daily basis, often without realizing it. It will show you how to recognize those influences and counteract them and how to reclaim and creatively express the power and essence that is the true you!

PART I: REMOVING THE VEILS

PART I:

Removing the Veils

You should investigate something to see its benefit or harm, examine whether it is appropriate or suitable or not; then after that you may carry it out.

Caotang

Thank you for buying this book. If you would like to receive any further information about our product list, please return this card after filling in your areas of interest.

Title of this book...

If purchased : Retailer's name............................Town.........
....

☐ Health and Nutrition   ☐ Philosophy & Spirituality
☐ Indigenous Cultures   ☐ Psychology & Psychotherapy
☐ Occult & Divination   ☐ Women's Interest
☐ Personal Growth   ☐ Other

Name..
Address..
....

DEEP BOOKS LTD
UNIT 3 GOOSE GREEN TRADING ESTATE
47 EAST DULWICH ROAD
LONDON
SE22 9BN
UK

Chapter 1

The Truth About Psychic Protection

Can it really be said that before the day of our
pretentious science, humanity was composed
solely of imbeciles and the superstitious?

R.A. Schwaller de Lubicz

In this wonderful time to be alive, we have more knowledge of the mysteries of Nature than at any other time in human history. Much of what used to be scoffed at by the scientific community now has to be re-examined in the light of modern metaphysics. We know more about the human essence and its abilities than ever before. We know that the human body is a biochemical, electromagnetic energy system with the ability to affect and be affected by much more than what was ever believed.

The once theoretical atom is today a scientific reality, and we understand more about the psycho-structure and potentials of the human mind than ever imagined. The scientific realms are aligning with the alchemical.

Knowledge of every aspect of human life, physical and spiritual, is plentiful today. Mystical knowledge, magical teachings, and spiritual revelations are being re-examined and understood in the light of modern science, and this information is available to the general public as never before.

At some point within our growth and evolution, all of this information helps us discover there is more to life and to ourselves than what is tangible and visible. We begin to realize we are energy itself with all of its inherent possibilities.

When we break matter down to its atomic and its subatomic levels, we discover that the atoms which comprise the cells and molecules of all life are not solid at all. These atoms are comprised of electrons and protons, subtle energy fluctuations that are in constant movement. The manner in which they come together, like bands of energy linking, forms the infinite varieties of all life and matter.

In essence, everything is energy and cannot be destroyed; but energy can be altered, directed, and even transformed by a variety of influences. If we are not conscious of this, our own essence, our energy systems may be altered, directed, and even transformed in subtle but very real ways.

Modern science is frequently demonstrating how we are affected by unseen influences. Sound is an energy wave that impacts upon and influences our energy essence and has the potential of altering and affecting our health for good or for bad, often without our recognizing it. Although we cannot see sound, most of us can recognize that sounds can soothe or excite us.

For example, sound volume has been acknowledged as a contributing cause to a multitude of physical and emotional imbalances and diseases. The decibel is the unit of measure-

MAGIC AND SPELLS

This series of three prints, which seems to represent straight magic to us now, probably stood for a fairly critical sort of scientific exposition in its own era, which was about 1600. (Don't look now, but much of the best scientific theory of today will seem similarly magical in time.)

The prints are the work of Raphael Custodis, a German who lived in Augsburg, and died in Frankfurt in 1651. He came from a family of printers, his father being Dominick Custodis, born 1650; a son of Peter Balten; Dominick took the

name Custodis in 1584. The plates are marked "Stephan Michelspacher Ex.," but we have not so far been able to throw any light on him.

In the prints there are references to the elements then recognized, Earth, Air, Fire, and Water, also to Ammonium, Sulphur, Bismuth, and Vitriol; the disciplines of Astronomy, Philosophy, and Alchemy are happily linked.

OCCULT DIAGRAMS

These diagrams illustrate alchemical and occult mysteries.

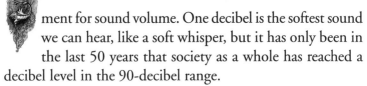

ment for sound volume. One decibel is the softest sound we can hear, like a soft whisper, but it has only been in the last 50 years that society as a whole has reached a decibel level in the 90-decibel range.

Decibels increase on a logarithmic level. In other words, 10 decibels is 10 times greater than one decibel, but 20 decibels is 10 times greater than the 10 decibel range, or 100 times greater than that initial whisper. One hundred decibels are a billion times as intense as one decibel. The 90-decibel level of modern society is equivalent to the sound of one train pulling into a subway station. One hundred decibels is equal to the sound of 10 trains pulling, while 110 decibels is equal to the sound of 100 trains arriving. Most of us are being exposed to sounds in this range at some point each day. The effects can be quite detrimental, accumulating, and creating increasing stress upon us and our energy systems.

Just as every cell within the human body is a sound resonator, with the ability to respond to all sound intensities, the human essence can also respond to all other subtle influences. These include, but are not limited to: electricity, magnetic substances, aromas, light frequencies, chemicals, thoughts, and even those energies of other realms that we classify as spirit.

Therefore, when I speak of psychic protection, I am not referring just to the strange forms of psychic phenomena so often depicted falsely by the entertainment industry; I am referring to the protection and balancing of *all* energies that comprise our psyche. This includes protection of our physical, emotional, mental, and spiritual energies from any extraneous and harmful influences.

Everyday our body, mind, and spirit are impacted by subtle influences, many of which we may not be aware of.

THE PURPOSE OF THIS BOOK IS THREE-FOLD

1. It will serve as a manual of psychic principles and common-sense practices that anyone can use for better health, balance, and discernment in today's world, especially those who are working within the metaphysical, holistic, and psychic realms.

2. It will dispel the myths, misconceptions, and unfounded fears of unseen influences, including those we classify as ghost or spirit.

3. It will provide practical, scientific, and spiritual tools for protecting our environment, our lives, and ourselves.

Advertisers combine sound and images to move us emotionally, persuading us to purchase their products. Stores use fragrances to manipulate our minds and emotions, to make us feel at ease about purchasing.[1] Politicians use rhetoric and carefully crafted imagery to sway our votes. We all experience pressures at home, school, or at work. Daily we are bombarded by sound, light, and even electrical frequencies that are discordant with the body and mind, creating stresses that can eventually manifest dis-ease and imbalance.

Many of these influences are capable of aggravating or even creating serious health problems on physical, emotional, mental, and spiritual levels. If we remain unaware of how extraneous forces impact upon us, of how these stresses accumulate, we will easily see ourselves, our environments, and our lives disrupted and unbalanced.

Benefits of Psychic Protection

Everyone can benefit from psychic protection. Through sickness, daily stresses, and outside influences, anyone's natural defenses and resistance can be lowered. Anyone who is ill can benefit from the exercises and techniques in this book for strengthening the aura and thus overall vitality.

Healers, psychics, and teachers need to be able to keep their energies at a high level to be effective and to prevent being drained by their clients and students. The techniques will help you work more clearly with those who seek out your skills and services.

---

[1] This is most noticeable around Christmas when many stores use the "traditional" bayberry fragrance, a fragrance that eases worries and doubts, including worry about overspending and finances.

Individuals developing their psychic abilities can use the techniques in this book to help keep themselves balanced and more discriminating in their abilities as they open up to the subtle realms. Individuals who are sensitive will find themselves stronger and less easily influenced through the techniques in this book. Those believing themselves manipulated or attacked (whether real or imagined) will find that these techniques dissipate unwanted influences and help build up energy reserves so as to be less affected in the future.

Those in the business world are subject to stresses unique to the work environment. Techniques in psychic protection will enable you to be more productive by increasing your energy and also by making you more effective in dealing and relating with others.

People in counseling or social work are likely to find themselves emotionally and physically drained at times. Anyone in the health care industry needs to keep energies vibrant and at high intensities, and thus all can benefit from techniques of psychic protection. These tools and techniques will enable workers to be more effective and will help prevent taking the work stresses home with them.

The primary caretakers of children, and parents in general, need to learn techniques of psychic protection since they are responsible for the creative development of children. Because of the family's demands upon them, along with the advertising influences and sales pressures parents are exposed to, the psychic protection techniques can help them make the home environment safer and more peaceful.

Even children can benefit from techniques and tools of psychic development provided within this book. Children have their own unique stresses. Since they are naturally open and psychic, these techniques and tools can help them develop

TEACHINGS OF GAUTAMA BUDDHA

Do not believe in what you have heard; do not believe in traditions because they have been handed down for many generations; do not believe anything because it is rumored and spoken of by many; do not believe merely because the written statements of some old sage are produced; do not believe in conjectures; do not believe in that as a truth to which you have become attached by habit; do not believe merely on the authority of your teachers and elders. After observation and analysis, when it agrees with reason and is conducive to the good and benefit of one and all, then accept it and live up to it.[2]

---

[2] Quoted in Max Muller, *Three Lectures on the Vendanta Philosophy* (London: Longmans, Green and Co., 1984).

　　　　　　　PART I: REMOVING THE VEILS

greater balance and less fear when experiencing psychic phenomena. Parents, teachers, and society as a whole place many demands upon children, and the techniques can help them to sleep more peacefully, to be more creative, and to be healthier, physically and emotionally, while meeting those demands.

Psychic protection is not just for those in the psychic and metaphysical field. True psychic protection is essential to the health and well being of everyone. Control of our environment begins with control of our own energies. We cannot influence our environments until it ceases to influence or control us. This is accomplished through increased awareness of our energies and their potentials, by strengthening and directing them on all levels and by working with the natural laws by which all life operates.

When we have better control of our environment, there is a natural rhythm and flow to life. Obstacles are easier to overcome, and each year brings new creativity and growth. We still must work and put forth our energies, but we find the walls and hindrances dissipate more quickly and easily. Tasks are accomplished more readily. Everything becomes more inspired. We once again remember that magic and miracles are real, and that life truly does work!

As a result of these exercises and techniques, you will find yourself more confident in handling the daily stresses you encounter. You will not only recognize them more easily, but you will be able to counteract them more effectively. The changes and contradictions of life will no longer be able to overwhelm you.

The Importance Of Knowledge

At any psychic fair, holistic expo, or metaphysical gathering, we can find individuals performing a variety of activities that range from the pleasant to the bizarre. People can be found drumming, smudging, chanting, and praying. These and a variety of other activities are used to prepare and purify the environment, "to raise the energy," and "to open to higher forces." All are nice colorful phrases, but what do they mean and how do these various activities accomplish these things? Many practitioners have difficulty explaining how they work, relying on the common phrase, "it just feels right to me" to describe their methods.

That is all well and good, but there reaches a point when we must get past the vagarisms of spiritual activity. We must bring it down to earth, striving to make the spiritual pragmatic and easier to understand. This means we must eliminate the many myths and misconceptions surrounding spiritual practices, and knowledge is critical to this.

The one area of spiritual practice currently creating a heated debate is psychic protection. Nowhere is this more evident than among the actual workers in the psychic or spiritual field. Psychics and healers often talk about surrounding themselves in white light, smudging, putting out healing stones and crystals, saying special prayers. Even among the workers in the metaphsical field, there is a great disparity of opinions in regard to these and other psychic protection techniques.

One faction approaches psychic protection with a fear-based response, in which the individual places the focus upon oneself rather than the client with whom he or she may be working. The other main faction promotes the idea that if you don't practice psychic protection, your energy will not be as high, you won't be as effective in your work, and you are ultimately inviting trouble. Such possible troubles range from emotional imbalances to spirit attachments.

As with most things, the truth lies somewhere in between. The first thing we should examine is why we perform these particular activities. Are they merely rote activities we perform because they are what we were taught? Do we know what they actually do, if anything? Is their practice just a modern form of superstition, a practice similar to "knocking on wood"? Are we performing them out of fear? Are we performing them just for an effect, to lend an air of exotic mysticism to what we are doing and ourselves?

Or is it possible that by performing such activities, we create a shift in our consciousness and our physiology that enables us to accomplish more? Maybe it's like taking a shower, putting on fresh clothes, and preparing for a job interview. We make a better impression if we are clean and dressed nicely when we go to an interview. The people we encounter will have more confidence and trust in us. A clean home (physically and spiritually) reflects a grounded, stable, capable individual.

Still there are those who will say that there is no need for protection as long as they open themselves to the love of spirit, to be a channel of light. This is a wonderful idea, but we live in a physical world that doesn't always play strictly by those rules. We are spiritual beings in a physical body and thus there are both natural laws and principles that must be considered along with the spiritual laws and principles because the two come together in us. Learning to work with both is part of our growth and responsibility.

Many workers in the field can often be heard making such comments as, "I have my spirit contacts, and that is all I need. They will protect me." Others say, "I use white light and so nothing else can affect me." Periodically I will even hear, "I lead a spiritual life, so I don't have to worry." Often the individuals making these comments have personal habits that promote and demonstrate physical, emotional, and mental imbalances. Since each aspect of ourselves is linked to all of the others, one unbalanced area of our life will affect the balance and health of other areas.

Everyone can benefit from a good health regimen, physically and spiritually. It doesn't mean that we must become ascetic and monk-like. Instead, by understanding some basic principles and incorporating some preventive maintenance, our vitality can be increased and our creativity strengthened, which facilitates our ability to manifest our innate potentials.

The Alchemist

There are just as many methods of protecting ourselves as there are people. Part of our responsibility is to find the method or combination of methods that are effective and work best for us and for the situation at hand, including those methods in which we find comfort and peace. This means we must prepare ourselves. Preparation always begins with intent and is empowered through knowledge.

Knowledge is critical to our overall health and balance. Just as knowledge of proper diet will help us in strengthening the body and preventing illness, a basic knowledge of energy principles and physics helps us to understand how our body responds to outside influences for good or bad. Knowledge of psychology reveals how the mind can be affected by outside forces. Knowledge of the ancient traditions helps us to dispel the many myths and misconceptions that abound in our modern religious and societal practices.

Throughout this book we will work to examine and eliminate some of the more common myths and misconceptions about psychic protection and the spiritual or psychic path. We will learn a variety of tools to help us against the many subtle influences we experience daily. Most of these are preventive, things we do to keep ourselves spiritually healthy. They are as critical to our well being as a proper diet, fresh air, and exercise. We will learn to discern and test things of a psychic and spiritual nature so that we can explore them safely. As a result, we will be more vibrant and more creative in all areas of our life.

Chapter 2

Myths and Misconceptions

*Anyone who proposes to do good must not expect people
to roll stones out of his way, but must come to accept
his lot calmly, even if they roll a few more upon it.*

Albert Schweitzer

The psychic field abounds with misconceptions, myths,
half-truths, unverified channelings, and general misinformation. Much of this has do to with ideas promoted
through the entertainment industry. Books and movies
promote concepts and ideas that are frequently not well
researched and usually half-truths at best.

There also exists the idea in modern society that if something is in print, especially in the non-fiction realm, then it
must be true. Desiring something to be true and its actual
validity are often quite distant from each other. Such perceptions lead to dabbling, insufficient preparations, and ultimately

to a variety of problems down the road, especially for those who immerse themselves in the world of psychic phenomena and all of its varieties.

Ten Major Myths and Misconceptions

Most people run into difficulties when they have dabbled or experimented without proper knowledge and preparation, or because they bought into one of the major myths and misconceptions surrounding spiritual exploration. In my travels, and with the thousands of people I teach and lecture to every year, I hear ten myths and misconceptions that are the most common causes of problems and imbalances for those already within the psychic and spiritual field and for those just beginning their explorations.

The problems that arise from these myths and misconceptions are easily corrected with a little knowledge and its proper application. Therefore, we must begin by through exploring and dispelling these common myths and misconceptions about the psychic and spiritual world.

MAJOR MISCONCEPTIONS AND
HALF-TRUTHS OF THE SPIRITUAL PATH

1. As long as I have my vision, all will be divinely protected.

2. I developed my abilities in a past life, so I don't have to worry about the development stages in my present life.

3. I must follow what my spirit guides (angels, guardians, etc.) say; they know better for me. I should just accept their promptings for they are in spirit.

4. Things of the spirit cannot be tested, so I should just accept.

5. I have my guides and my psychic perception, that is all I need to keep balanced, grow, and evolve.

6. I've developed my psychic ability, so now I am qualified to teach.

7. I have to be working in the metaphysical or spiritual field or I won't be growing or evolving spiritually.

8. If I'm suffering and struggling, I must be growing spiritually. Problems and difficulties are signs of clearing out spiritual obstacles.

9. Others are able to do psychic or spiritual activities because they are more naturally gifted. They are just part of the special few. Because of this, they also know better for me.

10. Once I find my spiritual purpose, everything else in my life will fall into place.

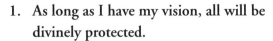

1. **As long as I have my vision, all will be divinely protected.**

Since the mainstreaming of everything New Age in the past decade, I have seen many individuals start centers, open book stores, and hang up their shingle for psychic counseling and teaching. Many of the stores and centers closed within several years. Many of the individuals who became professionals in the psychic or spiritual field struggled financially, having to return to more mainstream occupations.

With so many of them, I frequently heard, "I had this vision, and I acted on it. Everything fell into place initially, but then it all dried up." It is not unusual to see visions collapse once initiated. The vision may have been true, but a vision is not a guarantee. It reveals possibilities, but vision also demands preparation.

There is a certain level of glamour attached to working in this field, but it is a business, no matter how spiritual our practices may be, how strong our visions are, or how great our intention is. To make a living in any field of endeavor requires preparation and practical business skills. There are many pragmatic, often common-sense reasons why individuals do not succeed. Most center around over-reliance on the vision to protect them and carry them through. It all begins with realizing that the vision only reveals the possibilities, but it is still up to the individual to lay the foundation and to build upon that vision.

2. I developed my abilities in a past life, so I don't have to worry about the development stages in my present life.

It's amazing how frequently I hear statements like this. There are several fallacies with such statements. The first problem is that the individual making such statements does not really understand reincarnation. A little research into the lives of the ancient masters, most of whom believed in reincarnation, will reveal extensive study and development by them. We may have learned to read in many life times, but we still had to learn the alphabet, understand phonics, and develop a vocabulary before we could read in this life.

Some people even try to make themselves out as special or as the spiritual exception. The idea of being "gifted" is often abused. We all have the natural abilities and were gifted with innate psychic potentials, but we each must learn to develop them and apply them uniquely within our own life. Everyone has psychic ability, but only when we develop it and learn to apply it creatively and effectively within our daily lives does it become a gift. As we develop our gift and give to others, only then do we create the blessings in our lives.

If an individual tells you that they were "born" psychic, remember that so were you! If they tell you they are able to do what they do because they are just naturally gifted, or developed their skills in a past life, or because of an accident, or even from a near death experience, it does NOT mean that what they say is true or that they are any more spiritually aware or psychically developed than anyone else.

Regardless of the source of the "psychic gifts," they still must be applied effectively, accurately and responsibly.

An individual may have great psychic or intuitive abilities, but if they do not know how to present their insight in a manner that is helpful and effective for the individual, their gift is merely an underdeveloped psychic potential.

3. I must follow what my spirit guides say; they know better for me because they are in spirit.

We will examine the problems with this idea in much greater detail in Chapter 3, but the main problem with this concept is the assumption that spirit is synonymous with being more highly evolved. Think of water. In its densest form, it is ice; in a less substantial form, it is steam. Regardless of the form, it is still two parts oxygen and one part hydrogen (H_2O).

We are spirit in a physical body—our densest form. Our guides are just another expression of their essence, but less substantial than we are. Just as there is a variety of life in the physical with varying levels of development, there is also a variety of life in the spiritual with varying degrees of development.

Death does not necessarily make us any wiser. Just because a loved one or a guide is in spirit, it does not mean they know better for us. In the spiritual realm, there is development and learning just as there is in the physical.

The repercussions that come from following the promptings of spirit—good, bad, or indifferent—will fall upon us and us alone. Spirit does NOT always know better for us!

4. Things of the spirit cannot be tested,
    so I should just accept.

There are ways of testing and discriminating with things of spirit as there are with things in the physical. Throughout this book we will discuss a variety of these ways, from testing the spirits to determining true and false psychic phenomena. Never assume that something cannot be tested. I still test the spirit guides I have worked with most of my life. I still make them prove themselves to me by asking them to find me parking spots and to perform other simple mundane tasks.

Our true guides and teachers (physical and spiritual) will not be bothered or offended by our testing. If offense is taken and demonstrated, it is a signal that something is wrong. Our true guides and teachers recognize that as humans we need confirmation and assurance to develop and sustain our faith and trust.

In the modern world, we are often imprinted with the idea of accepting things on blind faith. It is not unusual to feel as if something is wrong with us if we cannot accept some things on blind faith. Faith is never totally blind, and we can maintain reservations until we feel comfortable or until we have enough information to go forward.

If something makes us feel uncomfortable, whether it is the presence of spirit or something told in a psychic consultation, HONOR THAT FEELING! NEVER ACCEPT BLINDLY! It is only when we don't honor our own impressions that we most often find ourselves in difficulty.

5. I have my guides and my psychic perception. That is all I need to keep balanced, grow, and evolve.

Developing spirit contact or intuition is not in and of itself going to keep us balanced. This is like saying that a basketball player's ability to shoot a foul shot reflects how balanced and spiritual he or she is. Spirit perception and psychic ability are learned skills, like shooting a basketball, and they reflect neither our balance nor our spirituality.

There are many things that can affect our balance on all levels. Our guides and psychic abilities may help us to recognize possible problems, but even then we must be able to discern and discriminate.

Psychic ability is developed, just like any other ability. It does not guarantee wealth, fame, or a peaceful life. Neither does it reflect a high level of spirituality. It is a tool that we can learn to use and apply to help us in life, but in and of itself, it is not a guarantee of balance or growth. It is often much easier to grow and maintain balance without the extra sensitivity awakened through psychic development. Being intuitive or psychically perceptive actually demands that even more care be given to maintaining balance in all situations of life.

6. I've developed my psychic ability, so now I am qualified to teach.

There are many things that qualify someone to teach, and development of one's own psychic ability is not nearly as important as some of the other skills necessary. A strong, solid educational base (formal and informal), the ability to speak effectively in front of others, the ability to demonstrate and guide, and the ability to counsel and serve as a solid resource to help others find their own way are but a few of the skills more important to teaching in this field than psychic ability.

I have seen many people develop their psychic skills, read a book or two, and then hang up a shingle to counsel and teach, spreading a great deal of misinformation in this way. Often poor preparation is more damaging than no preparation.

One of the best ways to develop teaching skills in the holistic and metaphysical field seems to be disappearing today. In the late 60s and 70s, study groups were common. These groups would explore many subjects, often remaining together for several years. The individuals of the groups would take turns leading and teaching.

We have seen study groups decline as the fast food approach of our society grows in its impact on this field. Many look for the quick and easy, ultimately shortchanging themselves and those they counsel or teach. Later in this book, we will examine ways of finding good teachers, psychics, and other holistic workers.

7. **I have to be working in the metaphysical or spiritual field or I won't be growing and evolving spiritually.**

This is a common false assumption. Many believe that if they are not ostensibly demonstrating their psychic ability or metaphysical education, they are not growing. As a result, there now exists a preponderance of individuals trying to teach and work in this field. Unfortunately, a great many have neither the depth of knowledge nor the experience to do so in the highest manner possible.

This is not to say that individuals should not strive to teach and work in this field. Teaching and sharing what we know helps us to clarify our own experiences and helps us to develop even more fully. What is needed though is an appropriate depth of background and schooling in the specific area and a well-rounded knowledge of the entire field of esoteric science. Without an in-depth background, it is difficult to discern what teachings to pass on, how to do it most effectively, and to what degree.

Teaching is not just passing on knowledge and information. It involves sharing in a way that helps others discover their own possibilities. It provides tools that will guide and assist the individual.

Many people can express knowledge on aspects of being psychic or on healing and spirituality, but it does not mean that their methods are appropriate or beneficially creative for anyone else other than themselves. Some people try to employ ancient methods, but many of the ancient methods of accelerating growth are no longer appropriate for our current times.

I have seen many teachers who are well prepared and quite excellent, but I have also seen a great many in recent times without a proper foundation of knowledge or experience. Many of the teachings are unfounded and a mixture of truths and false assumptions. This not only creates problems for themselves down the road, but also for everyone he or she has taught.

Although I am a good a writer, I am a far better teacher. My strong educational base includes ten years of formal teaching and counseling experience within the public school system, most of those years working with disadvantaged students who demanded even more from my teaching. Before and during those years, I also had many years of informal teaching and lecturing experience, honing my skills in people's homes and in study groups and wherever individuals wanted to explore the metaphysical. All of this was before I ever had anything published.

REMEMBER

If an individual is misled or unbalanced
because of another's teachings,
the teacher is responsible to that
individual and to every other individual
that the student in turn affected and
touched as a result of the teaching.

I still work daily to improve my teaching—assessing past presentations, practicing, rehearsing, and studying new material—preparing extensively for every class and presentation no matter how often I teach it.

Working and teaching in the field does not reflect one's spirituality or evolution. It is the fulfilling of daily obligations in a creative manner that propels us along the spiritual path. It is not the demonstration of psychic ability or book learning that unfolds our spirituality. In fact, such things can hinder our growth, especially in the early years of training.

Rather than focusing and concentrating on the new energy that is awakened, it is dissipated prematurely so the individual can place himself or herself in the public as a "teacher" or "psychic." The need or desire to be out front is part of what ultimately must be purged.

It is through the daily trials that we unfold our sleeping potentials. Through our struggles we can identify and then change outworn forms and patterns of behavior so newer and higher forms of our spiritual essence may come forth. For most people, this will involve simply touching and opening the hearts of others on a daily basis through a smile, a small act of kindness, or the meeting of obligations. Such individuals may not be demonstrating publicly their knowledge or acquiring attention, but it does not mean they are any less evolved or spiritual.

8. **If I'm suffering and struggling, I must be growing spiritually. Problems and difficulties are signs of clearing out spiritual obstacles.**

We live in a society in which the major religious influences promote martyrdom as the key to spiritual growth. I am a firm believer that suffering is only good for the soul if it teaches us how not to suffer again. We do not have to martyr ourselves to grow and evolve. Yes, we do have to put forth a great deal of time, work, and effort, and there will be obstacles within our paths periodically.

Obstacles are a natural part of life, and their presence in our life most often provides opportunity to develop our creativity. As long as we are in the physical, there will always be things we cannot control. These free variables of life force us to be ever more creative and productive.

I frequently hear two statements supporting and embracing personal suffering as a reflection of spirituality:

- *It's part of my spiritual initiation,* or in yet more recent terminology, *I am preparing for my ascension.*

- *Well, these troubles are just part of my cleaning out of old karma.*

I am always amazed at how often "bad karma" is confused with bad judgment. Progress and growth occur when we are in harmony with the natural laws of the universe, physical and spiritual. If we have been out of harmony with life, making poor decisions and choices, we are more likely to experience stress, turmoil, disruption, and obstacles. If we make appropriate choices and act upon them, applying appropriate efforts, obstacles and disruptions will be overcome and we will see discernible progress.

THE CONJURER
A milder, innocuous form of mass deception
not unknown in contemporary society.
(Painting by Hieronymus Bosch, 15th century German artist)
Courtesy of the Musée Municipal,
Saint Germain-en-Laye, France

9. **Others are able to do psychic or spiritual activities because they are more naturally gifted.**

Everyone has psychic ability. Each of us can develop it and learn to employ it within our lives. When we assume that others are more special and thus know better for us, we give away our own power. We lower our own self-esteem, and we set ourselves up for failure and dependence upon others rather than creating our own light.

If we give our own power over to others, we set ourselves up for many possible problems, perhaps placing ourselves in situations where we are manipulated and taken advantage of. Or, we may find ourselves victimized and entangled in things that can affect us on all levels, not the least of which is financial.

Some individuals may be able to express and develop their own psychic abilities more easily, but remember that it is like any learned skill, taking time and practice. As a reading specialist in the public school system for seven years, I learned that some may pick up reading more easily than others, but EVERYONE can learn to read.

Psychic skills are the same thing. Some may pick them up more easily, but anyone can learn to develop their psychic abilities or improve their intuition. Even if only developed minimally, these skills can enhance our life tremendously.

I know some very good psychics, but I would never go to them for a reading or consultation. Their ability to communicate is often askew, and their ability to actually guide the individual to find his or her own insight is limited.

Personally, I have not done any private psychic work for about five years. I believe in teaching others to do it for themselves rather than relying on someone else. I teach many seminars and workshops every year, and in the psychic development ones I present, I always do demonstrations since I am also a firm believer in the concept that if you cannot do it or have not done it, you CANNOT teach it. When working with others, my focus is to show them they can do it for themselves.

Ultimately, no one knows better for you than you. Development classes should help you to discover this. Yes, being human, sometimes it is good to get an objective perspective, but the more we learn to develop our own innate abilities, the less often we will have to depend on others. As a result, we become more productive and more empowered in all areas of our life.

10. **Once I find my spiritual purpose, everything else in my life will fall into place.**

Finding our spiritual purpose—like having a spiritual vision—is no guarantee of smooth easy life or the realization of that vision. Finding our purpose is not a guarantee that our life will now be so much easier, but it will give us motivation, something to work for while we prepare and act upon it.

The sacred texts of the world, along with most mythologies and histories, are filled with stories of individuals with a spiritual purpose or vision. Once found, their lives did not get any easier; many times their lives became even more difficult.

We must learn to prepare and pursue our purposes and visions appropriately, including any obstacles. We will have to put forth great effort, but we will see movement and growth if we persist. Often the work is just beginning when we discover our purpose or have our vision.

More important than discovering our spiritual purpose is having the determination to persist in the quest for it. This is where most people fail.

> Nothing in the world can take the place of persistence. Talent will not; nothing is more common than unsuccessful men with talent. Genius will not; unrewarded genius is almost a proverb. Education will not; the world is full of educated derelicts. Persistence and determination alone are omnipotent.[1]

---

[1] Israel Regardie. *The Complete Golden Dawn System of Magic.* (Phoenix, AZ: Falcon Press, 1984), p. xi.

MAGIC WINDS I
Witches were traditionally credited with the power of
bringing down the moon, changing the courses of rivers, and
creating storms. Olaus Magnus was a sixteenth century
Swedish chronicler.

Sources of Myths and Misconceptions

As we will discuss in greater detail later, true psychic attacks are rare. Most occult terrors arise from five common sources:

1. Stories in the entertainment industry such as books and movies (often resulting in an overactive imagination).

2. Superstitions which always are born from a lack of knowledge and understanding of the phenomenal world and the natural laws governing it.

3. Gullibility, which always results from giving over our own power or from ignorance. (Problems in this area often are the result of wanting to attain something easily and quickly.)

4. Propaganda from those wanting you to believe what they wish rather than what may actually be. (The belief in someone's ability to weave a spell or remove a curse is often nothing more than manipulative propaganda.)

5. Dabbling and thrill seeking in things not understood or by those who have a little bit of knowledge and experience and who mistakenly believe they are in control.

MAGIC WINDS II
In the Middle Ages, the belief in sorcery was so strong
that mariners, setting out on a voyage, bought favorable winds
from warlocks. Note three knots in the rope,
in which winds were allegedly tied.
Olaus Magnus was a sixteenth century
Swedish chronicler.

Common-Sense Precautions

Most problems in this field, and in most of life, are prevented through developing certain qualities and incorporating certain activities within our life. Most are common-sense practices:

1. First, take care of the physical. Keep the vitality and energy high through proper diet, exercise, fresh air, and such.

2. Try to develop greater strength of will and self-confidence in all areas of your life. These qualities make us more decisive.

3. Honor any feelings of being uncomfortable. Don't be afraid to examine what you feel and why.

4. Study. Educate yourself and explore.

5. Ask questions and don't accept anything blindly.

6. Seek out answers and explanations.

Remember that no one knows better for you than you, and no one is doing anything that you can't also be doing in your own unique way!

Chapter 3

Spirits, Ghosts, and the Unseen World

Fear always springs from ignorance.

Ralph Waldo Emerson

I enjoy going to holistic expos and psychic fairs. It is always fun to see what others are doing in the field and to be exposed to new ideas. Some of the things that show up at them are amusing, but its always good to keep an open mind.

Several years ago I was walking through the expo hall after presenting a talk on my book *Animal-Speak*. I went by a booth in which there was a man with all kinds of strange geometric devices and electronic gadgetry. As I passed by, he called to me and I went to his booth. As he shook my hand, introducing himself, he mentioned how he had enjoyed my talk, but then he added that he had seen something disturbing while I was speaking. I asked him what that might be, and in a soft fatherly tone, he said, "I saw about twenty spirit attachments."

I paused, smiling politely, unsure if he was joking or not. When I didn't respond, he continued. "If you want," he said, "I would be happy to get rid of them for you. I have a great device for that type of thing. In fact, with all of the people you interact with, it would be a good idea for you to have one of these to clean your aura of all that you pick up from them."

I stared at him, my smile frozen. For him to assume that with all of my writings, demonstrations, and teachings that I would be unaware if something had attached itself to me was rather disconcerting. For him to further assume that I would fall for such a ridiculous sales pitch was downright insulting.

As I continued smiling politely, I looked up and around me as if seeing all of these "spirit attachments." Then in my own serious, soft voice, I said, "Thank you. That's very kind of you, but it won't be necessary. We're all going out to dinner later." And then I walked away.

Nothing is more misunderstood and has more fear and myth surrounding it than the idea of spirit beings. Every society has had its teachings about spirits and beings less substantial than we are. From angels, faeries, and spirit animals to ghosts, ancestors, and even demons, mystical experiences involving the spirit realm are universal. When any teaching is that universal, it should make little bells go off, telling us something is going on here, something we should truly be paying attention to even if we don't understand it all.

The problem is that most of what people know about this realm has come to them through the entertainment industry: movies, TV, and books. In the past decade, aspects of this has bled over into the metaphysical and psychic fields. Today, at most metaphysical expos and psychic fairs, we often can find some people even advertising themselves as "ghostbusters."

Psychic trigger words, such as *ghostbusting, exorcisms, astral entities,* and *spirit attachments* are bandied about frequently. Most of these terms are misunderstood by the general public and disagreed upon by workers in the metaphysical and psychic fields. These terms tend to promote fear and fear responses, and I have a real problem with anything that promotes fear or uses fear to influence others.

The Phenomena Of Spirit

When it comes to the reality of spirits and their associated phenomena, most people fall into one of several categories. Some people assume all spirit contact is evil and will ultimately create many problems for the individual. Quite often these people believe all spirit contact should be avoided since to them it is merely a doorway to ever-increasing evil. There are always those who fear contact with any being outside of the physical. Often, because they do not understand, there is a hesitancy and a fear to explore or touch other possibilities.

On the other hand, there are those who believe there is nothing to fear about the spirit world at all; as long as they maintain their positive thoughts and white light, nothing can ever harm them. The truth, as with most things, is somewhere in between.

Experiences with spirit are not limited to seance rooms, old castles, or times past. Most people have had or will have some experience with this phenomena. Something will be seen when nothing is there. A voice will be heard with no one else is present. A feeling of someone standing behind or beside us is felt. The face of a loved one who has passed on may be seen in a mirror. The face of a deceased family person may appear in a recent photograph.

HOW SPIRIT MAKES ITSELF KNOWN

Spirit makes its presence known in a variety of ways, but we primarily experience it through the five senses. Unfortunately, the various phenomena of spirit often go unrecognized or are misinterpreted. The chart on the opposite page details some of the most common phenomena that people experience with the spirit world. Because such phenomena can have other explanations, it is important not to jump to conclusions.

Oftentimes the energy of a spirit is so strong that it triggers a physiological response within the body, stimulating an adrenal response. Adrenaline is the source of the body's "fight or flight" response in times of stress and emergency. Unless we are aware that the mere presence of spirit can trigger this, when we experience this flow of adrenaline, it is easy to misinterpret it as a response to something negative or evil.

The energy of spirits found within Nature often fit this category. They easily trigger this physiological response. It's not that they are negative or evil. They just have an intense energy about them.

Sometimes spirit manifests in other ways that can be misinterpreted. When my grandfather, who helped raise me, shows up in spirit, he comes in a cloud of smoke. He smoked Camel unfiltered cigarettes most of his life. It is this stale cigarette smell that his room always had that lets me know when he is present; my clothes and everything will smell like smoke afterward. It would also be easy for someone unaware to misinterpret such "clouds of smoke" as something evil or negative.

Spirit and the Senses

Sense	Common Spirit Phenomena
SEEING (clairvoyance)	Shadows and movements out of the corner of the eyes; faces and forms in mirrors, doorways, or windows; flickering lights of different colors; objects being moved or disappearing and reappearing.
HEARING (clairaudience)	Whispers behind you when no one is present; hearing our name called; house settling noises when it is not; music and singing from unidentified sources (especially when out in nature); ringing, buzzing, and popping in the ears.
FEELING (clairsentience)	Chills and goose bumps; changes in temperature; the fly-walking-through-the-hair feeling; adrenaline rushes; feeling of a spider web brushing over the face when none is present; changes in the air pressure around you; light-headedness.
SMELLING (clairfragrant)	Whiffs of flowers and plants when none are around; fragrances associated with those who are no longer alive and from which the source is unidentifiable.
TASTING (clairgustus)	Sweet or sour tastes in the mouth (not associated with eating or belching); tastes associated with one who is no longer alive (i.e., someone associated with a particular dish).

All phenomena of spirit are easily misinterpreted, and we do not want to assume that the phenomena automatically reflect a haunting, possession, or an unhealthy attachment. True phenomena of spirit should not be feared. Rather, they should be embraced with wonder and joy. They affirm for us the reality of life in all dimensions and remind us we are never truly separate from the ones we love.

Just because we have a particular experience does not mean that it is spirit-related. There are other forms of psychic happenings that can account for the most common spirit phenomena.

ACCIDENTAL AND PURPOSEFUL IMPRINTING

In my book *How To Develop and Use Psychic Touch,* I explain how objects and locations can become imprinted with an energy. We've all experienced imprinting before. Think about how your room felt different from that of a sibling or parents when growing up. We each imprint or leave traces of our energy that are unique to us. The longer we have an object or inhabit a particular space, the stronger the imprint. This is why, when we move, it takes time for the new place to feel comfortable. It takes time to imprint surroundings.

Imprints of objects and places can be accidental or purposeful. A purposeful imprint, for example, is the making of charms or talismans charged with a particular energy to elicit a particular result. Churches, temples, and meditation rooms are places where efforts are made to create an atmosphere of reverence or peace that we experience upon entering.

Accidental imprints are much more common. Places where there have been strong emotional events or objects held in possession for long periods of time become charged with a particular energy. Most haunted homes are not truly haunted by ghosts, but by imprints of events of previous residents. That feeling of discomfort in the home may be nothing more than an imprint and not an actual spirit. Using some of the simple techniques described in Part II, such as smudging, will eliminate imprints and help distinguish and clarify the presence of spirit.

When I first started becoming more public in my work during my college years and just after graduation, I began by investigating haunted houses. I was sure it was going to be exciting, one spooky thrill after another! It was actually the most boring work in this field that I was to do for some time.

A true investigation requires a great deal of study and research for other, non-phenomenal explanations. Is that door creaking simply because the hinges need oil? Does the door keep swinging open because the floor is uneven? Maybe the

Apparitions
A scene from Coleridge's The Rime of the Ancient Mariner,
alluding to the mysterious zones of beings beyond human familiarity. (Gustave Dore', 19th century French artist)

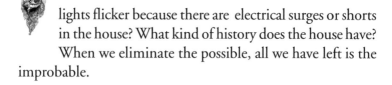
lights flicker because there are electrical surges or shorts in the house? What kind of history does the house have?

When we eliminate the possible, all we have left is the improbable.

Hauntings, Ghosts, and More

A true spirit phenomenon, no matter how strange, does not necessarily reflect negative forces at work or a haunting of any kind. Usually spirit will try to get our attention softly. If we are not listening, the knock on our doors of attention may get louder, but it is always important not to jump to conclusions or to make assumptions.

Much evidence exists to support the possibility of life after death. Some of the evidence is phenomenal and some is anecdotal. Around the world, ghosts are found to exist. Yes, the traditional ghost may be found in old homes, but in this country they are also found in southern mansions, modern two-story homes, apartments, and other dwellings.

There are homes with footsteps echoing, doors opening and closing on their own, and furniture being arranged. Sometimes the ghost appears as an apparition or as simply a dark shape. On some occasions, a voice is heard uttering groans and curses or sometimes fragrances are smelled and objects are moved.

Many strange phenomena exist all over the world. Some, if examined closely enough, have valid explanations. Others, even after careful examination, still go unexplained. Those that do go unexplained do so primarily for two main reasons. First, there is often a lack of evidence and understanding; second, distortion of events occurs because emotions—primarily fear—are involved.

It doesn't help us either that there is so much confusion surrounding death. It is natural for humans to fear what we don't understand. Even our major religions, which are the traditional authorities on death and life after, send us mixed messages and disagree about what actually happens. How often do we see priests and ministers speaking of the glories of heaven, and yet use terror of death and hell as a means of manipulating and controlling their flocks?

The possibility of the personality existing after death is often misunderstood, disbelieved, and scoffed at. In fact, all ghosts and spirits are often bunched together under the category of evil specters and demons out to frighten humans. This is the fodder of the entertainment industry and some religious groups and has little to do with reality.

The various beings of the spirit realm are viewed in a variety of ways. Besides being described as evil specters and demons, these beings may be described as lost souls, trapped in a nether world for homeless and lost beings. Reports of ghostly hauntings of homes and other locales range from mischievous, to harmless, to completely evil. Before we can determine what is true or false, whether a spirit is good or evil, we must begin by defining our terms.

Every society had its own way of classifying and naming spirits and ghosts. The following terms reflect the more common distinctions and descriptions. For the purposes of this text, I have kept these descriptions simple. I am aware that some sources have quite intricate and complicated metaphysical constructs and philosophies surrounding these entities and may consider my explanations as too simple and abbreviated. Others may disagree completely with my descriptions. I have chosen the most common terms that encompass most, if not

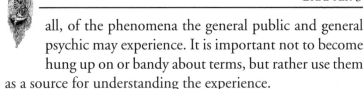

all, of the phenomena the general public and general psychic may experience. It is important not to become hung up on or bandy about terms, but rather use them as a source for understanding the experience.

ANGELS AND GUIDES

Angels are a part of most major religions in the Western world and appear in all religions and all literature around the world. Angels have become quite popular in the past decade, even among traditional religions and churches. This interest has served to open and bridge people to the possibility of other dimensions.

What is often called an angel may be nothing more than some other kind of spirit guide. A loved one who passed on and still watches over us is often called an angel. In addition to our loved ones, other spirit beings that assist us in some way are considered and often called angels.

The word angel means *message*, and thus any spirit being that brings us a message is technically an angel. For our purposes though, we will distinguish angels from other types of spirit guides and beings by defining them as a separate line of life, having bodies of lighter substance (often invisible to our heavier sensibilities) and who embody a creative and loving intellect.

A spirit guide is any being in spirit who serves as a guide or protector for us. It is often used as a general term for any spirit who assists. Spirit guides serve a multitude of functions, and we can have a variety of guides helping us within our lives.

A spirit guide may take a variety of forms. It may be a loved one who has passed on and is still watching over us or take the form of an animal that reflects the guides qualities and characteristics, or come in geometric shapes or a variety of colors. When a spirit guide comes in a form or appearance other than human, we must study its symbology to understand what role the guide is serving in our life.

Guides often communicate to us through our strongest sense or through the sense that will help us to recognize them more easily. Rarely have I ever seen my grandfather in a human form; I always sense his presence with the smell and appearance of the smoke associated with him throughout my childhood.

APPARITIONS

An apparition is any object, being, or place of supernatural origin. *Supernatural,* for now, refers to anything we do not have a direct scientific explanation for. It is a visual experience. Although often considered to be the figure or form of someone long deceased, it can also be the vision of an object, animal (such as a deceased pet), or even a locale.

The word implies the return of an entity to familiar surroundings, usually to accomplish a particular goal. This goal is often unfinished business, and objects and places that appear as apparitions usually reflect something unresolved. Apparition is often used interchangeably with the term *ghost,* and thus please refer to its definition as well.

ASTRAL ENTITIES

The astral realm is that dimension that reflects the physical, but is not as substantial.[1] The term is often used synonymously with spirit world. An astral entity is an entity, living

---

[1] This is a general definition. I am aware that some traditions teach various levels beyond the physical, including an etheric realm, mental realm, middle earth, etc. For our purposes, the astral realm is the generic realm of life beyond the physical, encompassing and intersecting the physical and other less substantial dimensions.

or dead, that does not have, or is separated from, its physical form.

The astral realm includes entities as diverse as the physical, human, and non-human. The human kind can be living or dead (as defined by physical life). The living are most often individuals who are still within the physical, but who are out of their bodies, and this usually occurs at night while they are asleep or through conscious astral projection.

Astral projection and out-of-body experiences are used to describe the time in which our less subtle aspects separate from the physical and enter into that less substantial realm. Unbound by physical limitations, this subtle body can travel to other places and times.

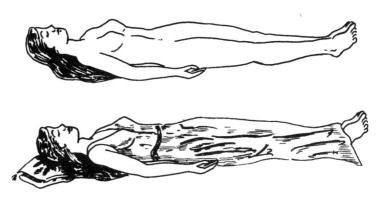

THE EXTERIORIZING OF THE SUBTLE BODIES
By going outside the physical body, the subtle bodies are able to more easily shake off the debris of emotional and mental energies accumulated throughout the day. This facilitates the rest and recuperation of the physical body. Part of this shaking off is reflected in our dream's scenarios.

We are comprised of more than just a physical body. We have bands of energy surrounding and inter-penetrating with the physical body. They are part of our auric field we will discuss more fully in Part II. They are part of our essence. Although traditional Eastern metaphysics teaches that we have a number of subtle bodies, for our purposes, we will refer to them all simply as the subtle body.

The subtle body serves a variety of functions essential to overall health and vitality, filtering out other subtle realms so we can be more focused within the physical. It is our first area of sensing and protection for the physical body and draws energy from the earth environment into our being.

Our subtle body exteriorizes from the physical at night. The loosening of it from the physical during sleep helps the physical body to shake off the stresses of the day and revitalize itself. Without the encumbrance of the physical body, the subtle body can draw energies more dynamically from the universe so that when it reintegrates with the physical, the physical body is re-energized. Separated from the physical body, it is unbound by time and place, free to experience and register experiences of more subtle realms.

Dreams reflect a lot of this process and these spiritual experiences. We can also learn to keep our ego awake in the subtle body and experience those subtle realms more consciously. Those who have experienced lucid dreaming are experiencing a small aspect of this process.[2]

Some entities encountered are just the astral projections and out of body experiences of those who are living. There are also encounters in the astral realm with non-human entities,

---

[2] Lucid dreaming is a process where we become aware during the dream that we are dreaming and are "awake" enough within it to change it or re-shape it any way we wish.

including ordinary persons after their physical death or contact with those waiting to reincarnate.

Astral experiences can also include contact with what is sometimes called a *shell* or *shade*. This is the subtle energy left behind by a deceased individual as he or she withdraws from physical life, like an old cloak of the individual that will dissipate over time. This is often known as the "ghost in the graveyard" experience. Such experiences, although a bit unnerving, are nothing to fear or be concerned about.

Other astral entities can be individuals who may have lived upon the earth at one time, but now work from the more subtle realms to guide and assist those still in the physical. We may also encounter thoughtforms which behave similarly to an entity but are not actual ones. (Refer to the information on thoughtforms later in this chapter.)

Probably the greatest confusion centers around what are known as the *lower astral entities*. These are the entities that comprise the spirit attachments which are so often promoted in modern ghostbusting.

Lower astral entities are those beings (often earthbound) that inhabit places where coarse and vulgar habits and behaviors are indulged. These entities often participated in such activities when alive, and not wanting or not being able to move past them, they experience them vicariously through live humans. They draw energy from those participating in these activities and stimulate even more obsessiveness in them in a parasitic or vampire-type relationship with the living.

A common misconception about them is that if you enter an environment in which such entities are likely to be, because of the electromagnetic aspects of your aura and your vitality, they may attach themselves to you, feeding on your energy and stimulating your own participation in lower forms of behavior. They, in turn, feel even more alive.

The only ones who may have trouble with such attachments are those whose health is poor and whose aura lacks vitality due to drugs, alcohol, smoking, and the like. Children are NOT more susceptible to this. If there has been some recent major trauma or ongoing abuse in an individual's life (child or adult), any of the simple techniques described in Part II will correct and prevent problems. For a normal, healthy, and vital person, any attachment will be unable to sustain itself for more than a few hours. The stronger and more vibrant a person is, the less likely he or she is to ever have any encounter with these entities.

There are those who would like you to believe this is not so, trying to blame imbalances and troubles on lower astral attachments. These same people are also the ones who blame every difficulty on "the devil" or some other force outside of themselves for everything that happens or doesn't happen within their lives.

Bogey Men

This is a name for any entity that is frightening or tormenting. Most ghost stories and movies center around this particular aspect of the spirit world, yet this is the rarest of ghosts, the least likely to ever be experienced, even by those who are dabbling.

One form of bogey man was the *ankou*, the graveyard watcher. In parts of Europe, when a new graveyard was created, it was customary to bury an unfortunate victim alive in the first grave so that a ghostly guardian was created. This tormented soul would frighten off others—alive or dead—so that the peace of the departed would not be disturbed.[3]

---

[3] Peter Haining. *Dictionary of Ghost Lore.* (Englewood Cliffs, NJ: Prentice-Hall, 1984), p. 6.

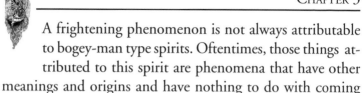

A frightening phenomenon is not always attributable to bogey-man type spirits. Oftentimes, those things attributed to this spirit are phenomena that have other meanings and origins and have nothing to do with coming from an evil spirit.

DISCARNATES

Discarnates are synonymous with ghosts, beings without physical bodies. They are incorporeal, and the term usually implies a human soul that has recently passed on.

Most traditions teach that when we die, we lay down our physical form. For a time during the transition from physical life to spiritual life, we maintain the appearance of that physical form, but the form is just less substantial.

EARTHBOUND SOULS

When my other grandfather passed away, there was no sign or hint of him at his funeral. I am sure he was so ready to pass on when death finally came, he was up, out of his physical shell and gone without a look back. He wasn't about to hang around.

My father, on the other hand, was very present at his funeral and for a time after. (Most likely to see who was going to show up.) But spirits that hang around for a time after death should not be confused with those who are earthbound.

An earthbound soul is an entity that has passed away in the physical but has not moved on to the spiritual realm. Sometimes individuals who die suddenly by accident, suicide, or with no preparation do not realize they are dead. Not realizing this, the entity remains among the living until realizing it is now spirit. The spirit binds itself to old physical life patterns, "haunting" the same places it did while alive, trying to do what

The Rebel[4]

When I
die
I'm sure
I will have a
Big Funeral . . .
Curiosity
seekers . . .
coming to see
if I
am really
Dead . . .
or just
trying to make
Trouble . . .

---

[4] Mari E. Evans. "The Rebel," *Our Own Thing* (Englewood Cliffs, NJ: Prentice-Hall, 1973), p. 156.

it once did. Sometimes this is accompanied by various corresponding phenomena, including the opening and shutting of doors, the sound of footsteps, and other physical manifestations.

There are a variety of techniques for helping the soul to realize its own physical death and to help it move on. Most of the time, this process will require little more than a some conversation and prayer.

Some spirits remain behind to comfort those that have been left. Others refuse to move on until the unresolved is finally resolved. Sometimes the spirits remain earthbound to inspire actions and thoughts of intimate associates. Others remain to help untangle mysteries and to pass on final messages. As we develop our own psychic and spiritual sensitivity, we can more easily determine why a particular soul has not moved on, and thus more easily help the entity.

GHOSTS

Ghost and *discarnate* are names applied to the often visible spirit of a person who has died. For our purposes, we will use it to represent any disembodied spirit. Most people at some time have an experience with ghosts—usually a loved one who has passed on. Although it can be unsettling when such incidents occur, it is not something to be feared, but should be embraced as a wonderful gift, helping us to affirm that we are never truly separated from the ones we love.

The conception of ghosts and spirits of the dead staying close to the earth should comfort us. Many times family members who pass away remain nearby to serve as guides and guardians to those left behind. They are usually recognized through familiar touches, smells, and even actual appearances.

Ghosts, the essences of those who walked the earth, do much for us. They show us there is no such thing as death.

They comfort us in our loss, and they often return periodically throughout our life, providing guidance and love. They will even serve as guides through our own death and through our own fears of it.

Often our fear of ghosts has its origin in reminding us that death separates us from those we love. Because of this, many souls remain earthbound for a time after passing to soothe and strengthen mourners.

Those who loved us do not stop loving us in death. It is common for the spirit of a deceased loved one to remain or return briefly to confirm this for us. Although startling, it is not an experience to be feared, but embraced with joy.

It sounds ghoulish, but I enjoy weddings and funerals. (Of course, the old joke is that they are one and the same.) I enjoy them because there is always a tremendous amount of spirit activity at both.

Several years before my father passed away, his sister, had died. Now she was an interesting woman. She always wore a very flowery, sweet perfume, and her lipstick was usually so thick that when she greeted us with a hug and kiss, we would smell like her the rest of the day, and it seemed to take forever to wash her lipstick off. My youngest sister particularly hated this, and would often hide when my aunt arrived.

At the time my father passed away, he and my mother were living in South Carolina. A small service was being held there, and then the body was to brought back to Ohio for burial. I was standing next to my sister in the reception line at the funeral home in South Carolina when I started catching the fragrance of my aunt. I smiled, recognizing it, and softly nudged my sister and whispered, "Hey, Theresa, smell that."

Theresa sniffed at the air, and her face crinkled. Without thinking she immediately wiped at her cheek as if wiping off lipstick. I had to laugh.

Yes, we do have to mourn the loss of loved ones in the physical, but we can also learn to embrace their new expression. We can remember that as long as we had love, they will always be a part of our life. We can begin to break down our fears.

NATURE SPIRITS

Nature spirits are those beings and spirits associated specifically with any aspect of nature. Every society taught that there were spirits associated with everything growing upon the planet. Every tradition had its own way of naming these spirits. In the West we most often refer to them as faeries and elves, but they are also called *devas, elementals,* as well as and many other names.

Nature spirits are Mother Earth's children. They are as many sided as nature itself, coming in a multitude of sizes, forms, and degrees of development and creativity. Every flower has its faerie, every tree its spirit.

Most of us have had contact with this realm without ever realizing it. If you've ever seen flashes of light around plants and flowers, you have probably had an encounter. Most traditions taught that to catch the fragrance of a flower or tree was a greeting from its spirit. Children's imaginary friends are often part of this group.

Nature spirits, faeries, and elves also like to get our attention. One of the more common ways of doing this is by moving objects around on us. Possessions disappearing and then reappearing are often an indication of spirit, usually nature spirits.

Nature spirits are often considered more ethereal than spiritual (ethereal being a midway point between physical and spiritual), since they can choose to be visible or invisible as they please. Their energy is frequently strong, inducing altered states of consciousness, and even triggering an adrenal response in the body. It is important not to misinterpret this response as a signal of something evil; it just reveals the intensity of their energy.

POLTERGEISTS

Poltergeist literally means "noisy ghost" and refers to activities and phenomena of spirit that are disturbing and usually distressful. These are the phenomena of unexplained noises, sometimes as simple as pops and cracks or sometimes as intense as possessions breaking.

There has long been great debate as to their true existence. Poltergeist activity often occurs in homes where there are adolescent children or children going through puberty, especially girls. One theory is that as the young child enters puberty, a tremendous amount of psychic energy (corresponding to awakening sexual energies) is released in an uncontrolled manner, resulting in the phenomena. On the other hand, some defend the idea that this new awakened sexual energy draws the troublesome spirits who further stimulate it.

There is a high probability that poltergeist activity is related to the sexual energy of individuals, either excessive, uncontrolled, or misdirected. The human body is a biochemical, electromagnetic energy system, and sexual energy is linked to our electrical aspects. As the sexual energy increases, so does our own electrical frequency. Poltergeist activity may be like an electrical short, giving off uncontrolled sparks.

More and more poltergeist activity is also being noticed in homes of menopausal women, a time when there is again a shifting in the biochemistry of the body and fluctuations in the sexual energies. This may stimulate uncontrolled release of psychic energy, possibly manifesting in poltergeist-like activity.

Regardless of its source, most poltergeist phenomena are eliminated through balancing the psychic energies and finding creative outlets for that new sexual energy. The best way to prevent poltergeist phenomena is by making sure adolescents and menopausal women don't dabble in psychic activities without learning proper techniques of balance.

THOUGHTFORMS

An old axiom teaches "All energy follows thought." Where we put our thoughts is where our energy goes. A thoughtform is a non-entity form of energy created through our thinking and emotion which often behaves as if it is an actual entity.

Thought is an outpouring of subtle force. If strong thoughts or ideas cause images to rise in the mind, this can create a thoughtform which becomes a floating form radiating a vibration. In other words, mental pictures can be artificially ensouled and become entities on the astral or subtle dimensions. They are sometimes called *artificial elementals,* and ultimately we are karmically responsible for all thoughtforms we create.

Thought has tremendous creative power in the process of what we manifest in life. The ancient Hebrew Qabala speaks of an aspect of the divine, *Jehovah Aloah va Daath*—God made manifest in the sphere of the mind. At the heart of the universe, at the heart of what we manifest, is thought.

If enough thought is concentrated and then fueled with strong emotion, it begins to take on a form, a life expression, and it will often show up in the aura. The form itself will vary according to the individual's focus, but it can take the form of ourselves, a material object, or even a form of its own. The quality of our thoughts often determines the color of the thoughtform. The nature of our thoughts will determine its form and the defined focus of our thoughts will determine its clarity.

If we have ever had difficulty severing or handling the severing of a relationship, we have experienced a thoughtform. This is most apparent during times of separations, divorces, and widowhood. When two individuals get married or have a relationship, especially in which there is sexual intimacy, a united thoughtform is created and strengthened. If divorce or death come about, the thoughtform can hinder the clean severing of the relationship. The two are often drawn back into repeated and unwanted contact, with neither party knowing why this is occurring. In part, this crrues because the thoughtform of the two is still present.

Groups use thoughtforms to promote their ideas. The stronger the group, the greater the thoughtform. This is part of what is sometimes called "group mind." I frequently hear stories of how groups are using magic and thought projection as a means of influencing and manipulating people and events. We will explore this aspect a little more fully in Chapter 4.

Thoughtforms are easily imprinted within homes, in objects, and in people's auras. Sometimes what people experience as a spirit is nothing more than a thoughtform that has not been dissipated, dissolved, or transmuted. Thoughtforms have dynamic electrical aspects and that energy can be the cause of spirit-like phenomena. Thoughtforms that are created must at some point be dissipated or transformed; if not, the thoughtform can become troublesome.

Thoughtforms are a product of our power of creative imagination. Learning to control and direct our thoughts, fantasies, and imaginings is part of what helps us to manifest exactly what we need or desire, enabling us ultimately to be the masters of our own destiny.

Spirits

A *spirit* is any being or entity that lives, works, and operates on a non-physical level. This generic term is often interchanged with ghost and some of the other terms described here. Spirit can be used to reflect angels, guides, beings of nature, and the souls of those departed from physical life.

Spirit Attachments

Spirit attachment describes a spirit of some sort (and sometimes a thoughtform) that has attached itself to the aura or energy of a living human or to a particular place. The relationship is often parasitic or vampire-like, as the entity draws upon the human's personal energies to give itself more vitality—to make itself feel more alive.

Spirit attachments are based upon the principle of "like attracts like." If we are involved in negative activities, it draws to us negative entities. If we visit places where negative activities occur, we are likely to "pick up" some of those lower entities that may hang out there. Although there are some who would have you believe that it is just that easy, it really isn't.

Problems with Spirit Attachments

We will be more likely to experience some difficulties with spirit attachments if we are unbalanced and in poor health, experiencing trauma or depression, or involved in unhealthy activities. As long as the we maintain good health, balance, and habits, we will not have ANY problems with any kind of sustained attachment. Even if we were to spend some time in an environment where lower astral entities may reside, just the mere process of taking a shower afterwards will usually cleanse any such attachments from our aura if we are healthy. The stronger and more vibrant our energy, the less likely we are to ever have any problem with attachments, especially if we attend to the guidelines suggested on the following pages. In addition, the exercises in Part II help us keep our energies at a high, balanced level, easily preventing and correcting any problem with attachments.

SEVEN KEYS TO ELIMINATING
FEARS AND PROBLEMS

1. Nothing in the spirit realm can harm us as long as we maintain control.

2. The spirit guide does not necessarily know best for us.

3. Test the spirits. Do not follow their promptings blindly.

4. We should never become overdependent upon spirit.

5. It is not important who the guide is, but what information comes through.

6. Possessions and attachments are extreme rarities.

7. We do not have to be unconscious or in trance to work with spirit.

1. **Nothing in the spirit realm can harm us as long as we maintain control and authority and as long as we approach it with some common sense.**

The key to preventing all troubles with spirit is remembering we control all aspects of work with the spirit realm. Most people get into trouble because they employ inappropriate techniques, they dabble, or they are thrill seeking.

If an entity demonstrates a quality that makes us feel uncomfortable or a behavior that is inappropriate, we should just dismiss it firmly. If we were to invite someone into our home and the individual disrespected us, spilled things, behaved inappropriately, etc., we would tell them to leave and not invite them back again. The same is true for working with spirit.

If we tell a spirit to leave in a strong, firm ,and clear voice, it will do so. On rare occasions, we may have to repeat it, but 99 percent of all problems with spirit arise when humans do not control or assert control over the relationship.

Again, I repeat,: we control all aspects of work with the spirit realm. If any entities display a quality or temperament we do not like, dismiss them. We do not have to tolerate ignorant behavior within our physical relationships and we do not have to tolerate it within our spiritual relationships either.

2. The spirit guide does not necessarily know best for us.

Just because a being is less substantial than we are, this does not make them more evolved. Death does not necessarily make us any wiser. The consequences of working with spirit will fall upon our own shoulders, and so we must develop a healthy and trusting relationship with them.

Working with spirits is just that—work. All good relationships require a great deal of time and effort before strong trust is developed. It takes time to find out another's strengths and weaknesses whether in the physical or spiritual world.

3. Test the spirits. Do not follow their promptings blindly.

Our true spirit guides will expect and accept our testing. They will be patient with us, realizing humans need a great deal to eliminate our doubts. Doubts and worries will not offend our true guides. If a spirit displays impatience, recognize that it is a sign of something being wrong. Dismiss the spirit because it obviously does not have our best interest at heart.

Ask your spirit guides for specific messages for friends and for yourself. It should be information that can be used and applied within a reasonable time frame. In this way, the information can be verified more easily. With new spirit guides,

I always ask for information that can be verified or confirmed several times within seven to ten days.

The time frame will vary according to guides. Always test several times. Don't draw conclusions from one testing. Not everything can be controlled or determined by spirit. If the information does not play out after several tests, the spirit guide is probably not legitimate and should be dismissed.

Ask for favors and assistance. Spirit can't do for you, but they can help. Periods of transition and difficulties can be excellent times to ask for some extra help smoothing things through. Ask the assistance to be brought to you through dreams. Ask for opportunities to be placed within your path. If something happens once or twice, you are still in the realm of coincidence. When it starts happening more than that, something else is at work.

4.   We should never become overdependent upon spirit.

When working with spirit, keep in mind that these entities are not around us to do everything for us, nor will they. They are not an excuse for inactivity either. I know individuals who are professionals in this field and who have been stuck in a miasma of continual problems because they will not change until spirit tells them it is O.K. to do so. We should never become overdependent upon them or use them to cure our loneliness.

There are many people who expect their guides to do everything for them. They even frequently use spirit as their excuse not to take action in their own lives. We should adapt the phrase: "The Lord helps those who help themselves" to "Spirit helps those who help themselves."

5. **It is not important who the guide is, but what information comes through.**

We should not parade our relationship with guides around for the benefit of our own ego. It is amazing how much name dropping goes on in metaphysical and spiritualist circles concerning spirit guides. So many want others to know that they are channeling spirits and who they are so they drop famous and exotic names to impress others.

Names of spirit guides are not important. The name might have been chosen because it is easier for us to remember. An individual who is channeling Jesus may not be channeling Jesus at all, but the name Jesus may simply reflect the spiritual quality that the human can relate to.

As long as the relationship is productive and beneficial, what difference does it make whether your guide's name is Buddha or Charley? What is most important is whether or not the information helps us to resolve issues and be more productive within our lives. If the work with spirit accomplishes this, then the name is irrelevant.

6. **Possessions and attachments are extreme rarities.**

Although many cases of possession have been reported and are often the subject of talk shows and movies, I have never personally encountered a true case of possession. I have been consulted and helped investigate a number of possession cases around the country, but I have yet to experience a legitimate case.

This does not mean that I don't believe possession can happen, but it is extremely rare. When and if it does occur, there is usually something in the physical which has occurred to make it possible: major trauma, abuse (drug, alcohol, sexual), inappropriate development (especially of trance work), dabbling in black magic, and similar activities.

Most of what the public knows about spirit possession comes from the movies and is completely false. As long as we lead a balanced, healthy life, we will NEVER have to worry over any such thing, even if we are working with spirit guides.

The entertainment industry has also fostered a belief that children are more susceptible to possession and attacks by spirit. Movies and books use children as the subject of spirit attacks because this taps into primal fears of adults and helps sell tickets. This perception is false!

Children have an extremely protective energy surrounding them and a strong light about them. Yes, they are generally more perceptive of the spirit realm, and most "imaginary friends" are not at all imaginary. Unless there has been some major abuse or something that has short-circuited within the aura and basic energy of the child, possession of children is next to impossible.

7. **We do not have to be unconscious or in trance to work with spirit.**

We do not have to be unconscious to meet and work with our spirit guides. In fact, it is best to always be fully conscious. Personally, I want to know what is going on. People frequently ask if I channel my books, and the answer is no. I research and apply.

No spirit uses my body. If the message is that important, our guides will find a way of getting it to us without our having to be unconscious. If the message is that important, and the guide can not get it to me consciously, then let the guide pay tax and title and come back into the physical with his or her own body.

I frequently hear people espousing that they have to let the masters use their bodies to work through them to get the message across. The problem is every master that walked the earth showed himself and herself to followers after death. They did not need another human's body then and they do not now. Most often those who espouse such activities are doing so to make themselves appear special.

There has been some wonderful channeled material in the past decade or so, but there has also been a lot of unsubstantiated garbage. The problem is that most people don't take the time to try and differentiate.

Many channeled communications are little more than empty platitudes. A lot of individuals jumped on the "modern spiritual band wagon" of channeling to get attention, employing pseudo-accents and proclaiming elaborate, unprovable sources for the channeled material, some with great success. But it doesn't make the information valid.

Channeling and Trance Work

Channeling has become a catchall phrase for a variety of psychic phenomena—from creative inspiration to spirit speaking through one's body while the individual is in trance. When the trance work is not prepared for appropriately, imbalances occur, usually rearing their head within three years, but always within three to seven years. Health problems will arise, emotional instability occurs, and personal lives become greatly troubled. Although some may tell us that it is just part of their spiritual initiation, it is a usually a reflection of inappropriate development.

When we open to the spirit world, we open ourselves to some dynamic energy. If we are not prepared for this, it can be like running 300 volts through a 110-volt outlet. The outlet may handle the current initially, but it will eventually short circuit and burn out. Many channelers have been and are currently experiencing this short circuiting within their lives. We will explain more of how this occurs and how to prevent and correct it in Part II.

> A trance channel is simply a person who has developed the ability to set aside one level of consciousness and allow another level of consciousness to come through.[5]

Traditionally there are two kinds of trance: mediumistic and shamanic. In a mediumistic trance, the individual learns to withdraw consciousness from the physical body, allowing a spirit to communicate through it or overshadow the personality of the individual.

---

[5] Kevin Ryerson. *Spirit Communication.* (New York, NY: Bantam Books, 1989), p. 5.

In shamanic trance, the individual learns to withdraw the consciousness from the body, leaving the body protected, and then goes out to communicate with the spirits directly, later consciously returning to the protected body. The soul, while outside of the body, explores other dimensions, communicates first hand with spirits of various sorts, and returns with full memory.

Shamanic trance requires much more development and skill than mediumistic trance. Shamanic trance is active, while mediumistic trance is passive. It is always more beneficial to develop and control our faculties than to simply sit, waiting to be used as an instrument. Consciously controlled spirit work involves taking our development directly in hand.

PART I: REMOVING THE VEILS

Chapter 4

Energy Drains, Group Mind, and Manipulations

*In every case, the remedy is to take action. Get clear
about exactly what it is that you need to learn
and exactly what you need to do to learn it.
Being clear kills fear.*

Laurence G. Boldt

N o word conjures up more images and emotional
responses than the word "magic." From sleight of
hand and prestidigitation to mystical talismans and
acts of wizardry, the word holds an ancient enchantment, hint-
ing of journeys into the unseen. At its root, the word *magic*
means *wisdom* and can be defined as a process to become more
than human, to unveil the potential that resides and operates
within each of us. Magic is not based on superstition or on
supernatural happenings. Things often seem supernatural
because they are not understood.

Magic, Jealousy, and Envy

Periodically I receive mail or calls from individuals who are "being attacked" or who are positive someone is using black magic on them. They seek an amulet, a talisman, a special prayer or bit of magic to counteract what they feel is creating the problems within their lives. I also come across those who were told in a psychic reading that someone has cursed them or is using *witchcraft*[1] against them. Often such statements are preludes to offers to counter the spells—for a significant fee, of course. Such statements play upon the ignorance and fears of the individual.

It is easy to blame life's troubles and problems on spirit, the devil, curses, or witchcraft, but blame makes us impotent. It promotes the idea and the energy that someone else can control or manipulate our lives. Yes, occasionally there arises a story of someone who has been "casting spells," but most often such public tales are propaganda, woven by the practitioner to impress and manipulate.

I frequently hear tales of great magical feats by individuals, but only in a very few rare cases have I seen such feats actually demonstrated and verified. Most often the individuals boasting of their work cannot even control their own lives, much less someone else's.

True magical attacks and manipulative spell work are rare. Yes, there are those who attempt it, but they are usually dabblers, trying to make themselves appear as something they are not. An examination of the lives they lead will reveal much about their "powers."

---

[1] The word *witchcraft* is often used as an emotional trigger by psychic hustlers. Witchcraft and its religioin *Wicca* both have spell work within them, but true practitioners are reverential in regards to the use and the repercussions of such activities.

Amulet Seller
Amulets were objects usually worn on the person as a protection
against black magic and its malefic effects. They were in use
from the earliest times, especially among the Chaldeans,
Egyptians, Greeks, and Romans. Roman matrons often used
such amulets or talismans as love charms.
(Painting by H. Slemeradzki)

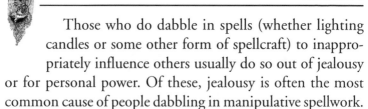

Those who do dabble in spells (whether lighting candles or some other form of spellcraft) to inappropriately influence others usually do so out of jealousy or for personal power. Of these, jealousy is often the most common cause of people dabbling in manipulative spellwork.

There is a tremendous amount of jealousy and envy found within the metaphysical and psychic field, just as in any other field of endeavor. It's as if people everywhere fear there is not enough abundance in the universe for everyone, but only for the few. Some psychics and metaphysical workers worry about who is doing what, how much they are making, and how much attention they are getting. I am always amazed at how much jealousy and manipulative spellwork is performed in spiritualist camps against other workers.

If we focus on improving our own work and on how we can teach and guide others more effectively, we will not have time to worry about others and how they are doing or how much they are making. We will be much too busy.

Those who are truly capable of such things are very aware of the repercussions, and so avoid all manipulations. They also go out of their way to prevent others from knowing what they can and cannot do. They are never found speaking of their spiritual activities except in special environments and circumstances. Humility and respect are their keynotes.

Later in this book we will examine ways of making sacred amulets and using prayers and words of power to enhance our life. We will also explain how these "magical" things work, which is not out of some supernatural conjuring, but based on scientific and metaphysical principles of mind, energy, color, and sound.

All magical systems, all philosophies, and all religions are nothing more than a system of props that strengthen and stabilize us as we open to new mysteries and until we discover the true power and magic of our souls. When that happens, every thought becomes a sacred charm and every word we speak weaves its own magical spell.

Energy And Psychic Vampires

At some point in our lives, we all experience being around individuals who "suck us dry" of our energy. We talk to individuals on the phone, we visit a family member, or have an acquaintance pay us a visit, and when it is over, we feel completely exhausted. We can feel as if someone has literally kicked us in the stomach or knocked the wind out of us. We may feel as if some vampire has actually had its way with us.

Such experiences are common to everyone at some time. If we are drained from being around someone, this does not mean that the other person was doing this intentionally or that the individuals involved are evil or negative. Nor should we seek out ways to have an exorcism performed upon them; however, we do need to acknowledge the situation and do something to correct it.

There are usually three origins of vampire-type of happenings, none of which are the Bela Lugosi type:

- living humans
- discarnates
- artificial elementals and thoughtforms

We have all had our energy drained. Sometimes this happens unconsciously; sometimes not. When it does happen, it is usually due to the qualities and characteristics of the human aura (the energy field surrounding the human body). We will explore all of its qualities in Part II, but for now it is

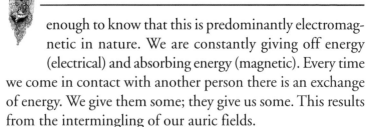
enough to know that this is predominantly electromagnetic in nature. We are constantly giving off energy (electrical) and absorbing energy (magnetic). Every time we come in contact with another person there is an exchange of energy. We give them some; they give us some. This results from the intermingling of our auric fields.

Living Humans

Individuals who "suck us dry" are often much more magnetic—which draws our energy away from us. This is a vampire type of activity in which we are drained of our electrical energy, not of our blood. We feel weak, tired, and even sick after such occurrences. Most experiences like this occur without the other individuals' realizing they are doing it. They may simply realize after visiting or talking on the phone with you that they just feel better—more energized.

This type of vampire activity is easily corrected. The exercise for the Posture of Protection described in Chapter 6 will eliminate this occurrence. This posture closes the circuit of energy so we do not exchange energy with others we are around or talking with.

Usually within a week or so of performing this exercise, we begin to hear statements like, "You know, Ted used to be so open, but now he is different." I may be just as open as always, speaking with them in the same way I always do, but I am just not allowing them to have my energy. It is our energy, and we should be able to consciously decide to whom we give it and to what degree.

ST. ANTHONY TORMENTED BY DEMONS
In all ages and countries demons were believed
to assume human or partly human form
in order to torment or tempt mortals.
(Tempera on wood painting by
Stefano de Giovanni Sassetta, medieval Italian artist)

DISCARNATES

Discarnates, or earthbound spirits, can also be vampire-like in that they use a living person's energy to help them experience what they no longer can. If we maintain balance and a strong vitality, we will rarely ever be bothered by such things.

There will arise periodically stories of spirits that have sex with humans. These spirits are more traditionally called *incubus* and *succubus.* An incubus was believed to be a fallen angel whose lust for women brought about the fall and who continues to have sex with women at night while they are asleep. A succubus was a spirit that assumed the shape of a woman for the purpose of having sex with men.

Belief in these entities arose at a time when the Church would tolerate no sexuality or thoughts of it. Sex was a grave sin. To blame one's desires, passions, and nightly emissions on an incubus or succubus was a way of avoiding blame by the Church. It relieved the individual of personal responsibility for a purely natural activity and response.

ARTIFICIAL ELEMENTALS
AND THOUGHTFORMS

Artificial elementals and thoughtforms can also be draining to us. Thoughtforms can become quite lifelike and may respond in ways similar to other energy drains. When thought is concentrated, it can become strong enough to take on a variety of lifelike behaviors.

Energy drains can occur easily, but they are not indications of psychic attack any more than a headache indicates cancer. As long as we keep our energies balanced and maintain a moderately healthy regimen, such occurrences are diminished tremendously. If we are aware of how they occur, we can easily correct and prevent them. Specific methods for this will be examined in great detail in Part II of this book.

Remember

Ultimately, we are karmically responsible for all thoughtforms we create.

Understanding the Power
of Thoughtforms

Thought is an outpouring of subtle force. If strong thoughts or ideas cause images to rise in the mind, strongly enough and often enough, they can result in a thoughtform, a floating entity which radiates a vibration. In other words, mental pictures, sometimes called *artificial elementals*, can be artificially ensouled and become entities on the astral or subtle dimensions.

Thoughtforms are part of the ancient magical technique of *weaving glamour.* Most people don't realize they are being influenced by thoughtforms even though all of us have experienced them at one time or another. Weaving glamour is the process of making something or someone seem like something they are not. Techniques of glamour can be used to disguise the negative and enhance the positive.

Some people use sex as a means of generating energy and creating more powerful thoughtforms. Sex magic and mystical sexual practices, unfortunately, are still often misused and misunderstood.

I once counseled a woman who had ended an intense long-distance relationship. Although these two people had never actually had sex, the two would schedule regular masturbation times and scenarios as a way of projecting energies to each other. Over the years I've encountered a number of individuals participating in variations of this type of activity. The sexual energy is our creative life force, and it can be a powerful tool for sending energy to another person if he or she is receptive.

When the long-distance projections ended, the woman continued to experience some of the phenomena of their activities. She accused the man of still performing the act—of projecting to her. She could feel him getting into bed with her, along with a variety of other sexual responses and phenomena. As she described what was going on, she mentioned also that the new experiences felt different from the past experiences: colder, with less vitality.

As it turned out, the man was no longer participating in the activity, but they had created a thoughtform through their fantasy projections. When the activity ceased, the thoughtform had enough energy—enough "life"—to continue on its own.

I explained how thoughtforms can operate, and I advised her to get rid of anything she still possessed of her partner in this activity. Then I had her stand on concrete in her bare feet for about an hour a day, three days in a row. This drains the energy from the thoughtform, weakening and diminishing it greatly. It's like setting a car battery on concrete. It doesn't take long before the battery is drained.

Once she had weakened the thoughtform in this way, I asked her to visualize herself drawing her own creative and sexual energy out of it completely, reabsorbing it back into herself. At the same time, I advised that she involve herself in strong physical activity for a brief time to ground the energy that was being reabsorbed. I also advised her to take up a new creative or artistic activity to transmute the energy. Within a week, everything was back to normal.

Energy cannot be destroyed, but it can be transformed. Over time, it will diminish in its intensity, but depending on the situation, the time involved can be very great. We must learn techniques for transmuting energy.

CHAPTER 4

CORRECTING THOUGHTFORM PROBLEMS

Most thoughtform problems are easily corrected. First, we must remember that at some point we are responsible for whatever energy we put out on any level. Even the negative must be neutralized, reabsorbed, and then transmuted at some point. Unless this energy is dissipated or transmuted, it may remain dormant or temporarily devoid of external activity, like a dead battery waiting to be recharged.

This is partly why coming across items such as old photographs rekindle all of the same old feelings. They can activate and recharge the thoughtform. Because of this potential recharging, as we will explain in greater detail later, it is important to retrieve all of your possessions when break ups occur and get rid of all photos, souvenirs, and reminders of the individual.

REMEMBER

The appropriate use of thought power
is to do no harm to any creature.

98   PART I: REMOVING THE VEILS

Thought has the ability to focus the energy that surrounds and permeates all life. In fact, because of this, the heart of our physical existence can be determined by our thoughts. We tell ourselves that we get two colds every winter. This sends a message to the subconscious so that as winter approaches, we are more susceptible to "catch" those two colds. Because of the ability of the subconscious mind to manifest, we create self-fulfilling prophecies.

It is for this reason that all of the ancient masters at one time or another urged their followers to learn how to control their thought process. All illness and imbalance—physical, emotional, mental, and spiritual—comes from a thought pattern that can help manifest the condition.

As we begin to develop our abilities and our innate energies grow, it becomes even more important to control our thoughts. Our new-found abilities accelerate their manifestation. There is a more immediate and powerful effect. There becomes less of a lag time between the thought and its manifestation because of new force.

Recognition of the power of thought has enabled people to utilize it in ways other than for spiritual development, leading to its abuse. So again, discrimination and understanding in the use of thought power is critical, especially for those who seek out psychics.

Psychic and clairvoyant ability does not necessarily reflect high moral character. There are ignorant psychics, mediums, and metaphysical teachers. Use discernment at all times. Rather than go to psychics to learn of spirit guides or other information, develop your own ability to perceive.

If you do go to others, there are ways to determine whether or not what you are being told or taught is mere fancy with a thoughtform woven around it and you, or something very valid. If valid, the information will be verifiable on some level. The teacher or psychic should be able to direct you to sources that will help you in your discovery and validation. Confirmation will come through outside sources and by events playing themselves out as told.

Most people, when they discover the power of thought in the manifestation process, fall into one of two categories when it comes to using it for material gain. One group holds that it is O.K. to use it blatantly to get what they want regardless of consequences. Others believe it should not be used at all, because one must suffer and be poverty stricken to be truly spiritual. As with most things in life though, there is a middle road between these two extremes.

ACCEPTING RESPONSIBILITY FOR
OUR THOUGHTFORMS

As we begin to grow and increase our esoteric knowledge, there is increased responsibility for its use. There are two ways in which esoteric knowledge can be used to better ourselves materially:

1. To influence the minds and wills of fellow humans so that they give us what we want (traditionally known as the way of black magic or the left-hand path), and

2. To use thought power to draw from the great universal reservoir of energy and abundance (traditionally known as the way of white magic or the right-hand path).

We do not have the right to interfere with the free will or responsibility of any soul. A legitimate use is one which brings harmony where there was discord. Some project healing energies without permission of the one who is ill, assuming that it is O.K. if the intention is good. We learn from all things—including our illnesses, and we should always have permission.

When I was doing individual healing work, I was frequently asked by individuals to send healing thoughts and energies to friends and relatives. Unless I specifically had an individual's permission, I did not do so, unless I qualified it with such statements and thoughts as "that this manifest for the good of all, according to the free will of all."

Yes, I did make exceptions in the case of children, especially whenever pain was involved. However, I did so in full consciousness and willingness to take on the karmic consequences regardless of what they might be—in this life or future lives.

When my father was first diagnosed with cancer, I directly asked him if I could do some healing work on him. He often scoffed and rolled his eyes at my choice of living, but he also never really understood what I do. He was so scared at the time though, that he readily agreed. His cancer was in recession for several years before it resurfaced. When it did, I contacted him again:

> "Dad, can I do some more healing work with you."
> "No, I don't think so. The doctors have it hand..."

It was from that simple statement that I knew he had made his decision. I knew he was preparing to die. It stunned me, but it was his choice. For me to send healing energies in spite of his refusal of my offer would have been morally and spiritually wrong. It was difficult not to do so, but even if I didn't understand the reasoning, I had a responsibility to honor his wishes.

This does not mean that we must be passive and complacent. We can learn to use our thought power in ways that will make processes in life—our own or those of others—more creative and productive. It means that on many levels we must learn to embrace life while not fearing death. We must develop a responsibility to the spiritual and the physical.

If we are unsure about sending thoughts and energy to others, even the healing kind, add the following to the prayers and thoughts:

> ...that this energy be used for the good of _____ and according to the free will of _____.

In this way, the energy can be used or not used by the individual we are concerned for. It is made available without intruding upon life's lessons or free will.

Group Mind

In the beginning, development and meditation groups can be a great benefit. All groups use thoughtforms to promote their ideas. The stronger the group, the greater the thought-form. This is part of what is sometimes called "group mind" or "group energy" that can accelerate development.

Metaphysical and occult groups will take on their own aura, employing group mind for good and bad. Ritual and ceremony intensely blends everyone's energy, strengthening the individual and group auras. This can create great harmony and

QUALITIES WHICH MAKE US SUSCEPTIBLE TO MANIPULATION

- weakened physical condition

- fear

- indecisiveness

- overactive imagination

- insecurity

- lack of knowledge

- guilt and other negative emotions

- blaming

- accepting blindly

- looking for the quick and easy

accelerated development of all members in the group, but remember that the group is only as strong as its weakest member.

If we are uncomfortable with a group after several meetings, leave it. Do not assume it will get better or that it is uncomfortable because you are new. Trust your feelings and go in search of a group in which you do feel comfortable. Many wonderful study and development groups do exist.

Cult-like Groups and Manipulation

Unfortunately, there are also a few negative, cult-like groups as well. Most people will never encounter them, but it is good to be aware of their existence. These negative groups usually have common characteristics. True cults recognize that if a change in behavior can be instituted, a change in basic beliefs will follow shortly after. I frequently hear stories of how groups are using magic and thought projection as a means of manipulating and influencing people and events.

This is often done through manipulating a person's imagination. Desire and fear are two of the strongest manipulators of our imaginative faculties. The group mind plays upon our inner desires, stimulating our emotions and it plays upon our fears, including the fear of saying "no" and the fear of missing a good thing. Some evening while watching TV, count how many commercials play upon our desires and how many play upon our fears.

When any group eliminates individual expression, warning bells should go off. If courage and personal confidence is frowned upon, something is wrong. If the group applies pressure to "get you to agree" to do something that you are uncomfortable with, beware! Group mind can be a means of controlling and sometimes manipulating individuals.

Beware of any group that wants you to make sudden changes in your environment, be it moving from your present residence or a change in job. Changes motivated by the group lead to even greater suggestibility and alterations within our personal belief systems. Beware of any group that pressures you into making important decisions without giving you time to think them through. Beware of any individual or group that requires absolute obedience, or makes claims of special divine connections or of special knowledge that can only be acquired through them.

If any group tries to separate or alienate you from friends or family, something is wrong. Beware of sessions that leave you exhausted or drained. Also, if there is a lack of personal privacy, take a serious look at the situation that is occurring. Always ask questions, no matter how silly or stupid you may think they are. I know it is a cliché, but there is no such thing as a stupid question.

Focus on your own activities and development and don't open yourself to personal confessions. Always maintain outside contact and work with the everyday world. **Cloistering does not enhance or reflect spirituality!**

Remember you always have the right to say NO to anything that makes you uncomfortable. Always make sure the group—and you—honor your own individuality.

Chapter 5

Psychic Attacks

Evil prospers when good people do nothing.

Edmund Burke

W hile psychic attacks do occur, they are very, very rare. By reading this chapter, you can gain a better understanding of the difference between psychic disturbances and a psychic attack. You will also learn more about the common indicators of a psychic attack. In the last two sections, you can find specific information about the types of things you can do to prevent a psychic attack or to lessen its affect if the need arises.

COMMON INDICATORS OF PSYCHIC ATTACK

- Characteristic repetitive dreams of terror and attacks, usually with similar scenarios and people.

- A feeling of weight upon the chest.

- Unusual fears and obsessions that are difficult to shake (keep resurfacing).

- Nervous exhaustion.

- Bad odors around all personal environments.

- Weariness around certain people.

- Depression and sleeplessness.

- Electrical problems.

- Temperature changes in home and other unexplained phenomena.

- Difficulties, trouble, and unusual phenomena around you, your closest friends, and your family members.

- Weariness (feeling drained) after being around specific people or situations.

- Symptoms lessen or disappear when out of the normal environment.

A Personal Encounter
With the Dark Force

Back in the early 70s I was approached for help by an astrologer friend of mine. She had been involved with a man from Texas for a while, but when she broke it off, he began to create troubles for her. Her nights were filled with terrifying dreams. She went through a series of illnesses, and her children were experiencing great problems and distress as well.

She suspected that he was the cause of much of this, because after every episode, she would receive a call from him asking her to reconsider and move to Texas with him. She asked if I would be willing to help her break the connection so that he would not be able to affect her psychically.

Having the arrogant impulsiveness of youth, I agreed, visualizing myself as kind of a psychic white knight going out to do battle with evil. I was sure I was skilled enough to handle this. Looking back, it was probably only sheer luck and blind ignorance that prevented my having more problems than I did.

I assumed this individual was someone who was all wind, who talked a good game of being psychically developed but really wasn't. I had already experienced so many of this type it was a natural assumption on my part. I figured it was all some amateurish manipulation.

I soon discovered that it was so much more. The man was actually part of a true occult group. Some people might call the group satanic, although even to this day I hesitate putting such a label on it.[1] They were very organized, very well

---

[1] The media often tries to blame satanic groups and cults for most unusual activities that have occult overtones. Most of the time the individuals involved are dabblers and thrillseekers and don't even have the basic knowledge of things magical or occult. This group should not be confused with those that often find their way into the media.

trained, very large, and very secretive. They were after power and control (spiritually and politically), and they employed ancient rituals, sexual magic, and other occult techniques. Needless to say, I soon found myself in a hornet's nest.

Within a month I was able to break the connection for my friend, but only with some most unusual help which I will speak of briefly later. I would pay a heavy price for my interference by becoming the group's focus. I ended up very sick, and although I was back to work within a few weeks, it would be almost a year before I found myself feeling healthy.

For the first time in my life, I completely lost interest in anything psychic and metaphysical. I wanted nothing to do with any aspect of the field and quit meditating, reading, and participating in anything remotely related. It would be almost two years before I would begin to meditate again regularly or study anything dealing with metaphysics once more. For several years after, whenever I started to make new strides in my own development, problems would arise. Health issues came to the forefront, along with a myriad of annoying distractions. I had succeeded in severing a connection between my friend and this group, but their anger at my interference was quite intense and quite tangible.

Although I debated even mentioning this episode, I do so only to let readers know that psychic attacks do occur, but they are very, very rare! Most of what people blame on psychic attacks has nothing to do with such things. Most individuals claiming such abilities are usually blowing smoke and feeding upon the gullibility and fear of others.

This is not a challenge for anyone to prove themselves or their "powers" to me. It is simply to remind those working in the field and those beginning to explore psychic development that psychic attack can be a reality, but there are much greater concerns to be focused upon. There are other problems more likely to manifest, other areas of the psychic and spiritual realm potentially much more troublesome and much more likely to be encountered than any kind of psychic attack.

Psychic Disturbances

Psychic disturbances usually arise from a variety of sources other than attack or intrusion. Psychic disturbances can be a by-product of physical disease and often occur at times of physiological change such as puberty or menopause.

These kind of disturbances can occur as a natural result of the heightened sensitivity during psychic development, sometimes occurring as a result of inappropriate development methods. They can be the result of non-human interference, of spirit phenomena manifesting around us. Finally, psychic disturbances can occur due to malicious human action—most of which fall into the category of manipulative thoughtforms and not actually true psychic attack.

If psychic disturbances manifest within our life, the first priority is always self-examination. What is there about us or our activities making us susceptible to the condition? Then we can meditate upon the compensating quality for the condition or weakness. For example, if we find ourselves infused with anger, focus on laughter and humor. It dissipates the anger, regardless of its source. We can rise above fear and nervousness by controlling the imagination. We can learn to rise above disturbances by meditating upon compassion and serenity.

Sometimes we must accept the conditions that have arisen. Realizing that all situations—good, bad, and indifferent—provide learning opportunities is the key to this. What can the disturbances teach us about our personal spiritual development? When we figure out possible spiritual lessons, we eliminate self-pity and resentment against our conditions, our fate. We break karmic bonds by working on causes rather than effects. By beginning within and then turning out, we empower ourselves.

If we try to discover what we are about in our present incarnation and if we pursue our true purpose with resolution, very little molestation, physical or psychic, will ever occur. The techniques and tools provided in Part II of this book will eliminate and prevent most problems that will ever likely be encountered by anyone working in this field or studying some aspect of it.

Psychic Attacks

In order to understand how psychic attacks work, we must understand some basic concepts. First, mental and emotional conditions have the power to affect us without overt physical action. We live in a time when we know that thoughts and emotions can trigger physiological responses within the body. Second, it is always important not to allow our reactions to subtle influences run away with us. Perceiving an influence is not the same as responding to it. We must first perceive something in order to counteract it.

DIAGNOSIS AND DIVINATION

Diagnosis always precedes treatment when it comes to true psychic attacks. This begins with our own subjective conditions. What weakness in ourselves has made us more susceptible to the conditions? Lack of endurance or courage? Lack of foresight or energy? Or is it a lack of self-respect?

How is our physical health? Are we eating properly? Are we getting exercise and fresh air? Are we using any drugs, alcohol, or tobacco which can aggravate conditions? Are we obsessing and stressing over things in our life, such as one's work, one's family, or one's career?

Have we been spending too much time on psychism and development? Psychism can lead to hypersensitivity and self-delusions if we are not balancing it with normal daily life activities. Many psychics are neurotic and have nervous disorders. Imbalances easily occur if we open up and develop our own psychic abilities too quickly. Causes for most energy drains and even "attacks" lie with the individual and not an outside source. Something that has precipitated or predisposed the individual to imbalances.

Meditation precedes any action or decision. This should not be a meditation upon the problem, but rather upon

Christian's Combat with Appollyon

spiritual development. It should be meditation upon dedication to the highest ideal.

The use of divination can assist us in determining diagnosis. Divination is a spiritual diagnosis whereby we try to discover what subtle influences are at work in our own affairs. This is very helpful if done correctly by an objective party. It can also be harmful if improperly done by depressing suggestion and sowing unwarranted suspicion. A purely psychic divination relies upon vision or communication from spirit. The use of divinatory tools (tarot, runes, etc.) helps to reduce (although it does not eliminate) the personal factor in the determination.

LESSENING THE EFFECTS

The key to determining psychic attack is to let reason, not emotions, be our guide. If we suspect psychic attack, we should get rid of unwanted images that can enhance and aggravate the condition. Remember that "All energy follows thought." We must control the emotions. Emotions fuel projections, giving them strength.

If we truly suspect a psychic attack by some person or group, we must first eliminate the more obvious possibilities for the discord or imbalance within our lives. Headaches and a general malaise don't always indicate psychic attacks. Other factors in our life might be at play. Are we getting proper amounts of sleep? Sleep is very necessary to avoid imbalances on all levels—especially psychic.

Are the problems in our life results of poor judgment? Are we taking control of our life's events or sitting back and letting events play upon us? Difficulties in life are not indicators of psychic attack. Most often they reveal something about our approach to life—something we are not doing and should be or something we are doing but shouldn't be.

What to Do If Psychically Attacked

1. Get the return of all personal possessions.

2. Be careful of your castoffs.

3. Keep information and plans about yourself to yourself.

4. Never accept gifts or hospitality from someone you suspect.

5. Avoid contact with the suspected party.

If we suspect that some person or some group is acting inappropriately towards us, there are certain things we can and should do.

1. **Get the return of all personal possessions.**

Our possessions are direct links to us, so photos, letters, and personal items should be returned. If this is not possible or the suspect does not comply, usually disconnecting yourself from the photo or objects is necessary. In meditation, see a link connecting you to all of your objects. Visualize the link broken, cut, severed, and burned so that it no longer links to you. If a photo, focus upon the fact that you are no longer the person in that photo; you have grown and changed since then. This may have to be repeated for several weeks, but it will usually break the connection.

If you have personal possessions or gifts of the other person, return them. If this is not possible, remove them from your premises entirely. They serve as a link to you, a doorway or window of projection for the other person.

2. Be careful of your castoffs.

Castoffs are personal aspects of you—usually your hair or nail clippings. These are sometimes called *witnesses*. Witness is a term often associated with radionics. It is "anything which will psychically represent the subject."[2] These things are a link to you. Again, it is always good to visualize yourself disconnected from them. They are no longer a part of you and thus cannot be a link to you.

One type of witness used by psychics is called a *billet*, an old spiritualist term. A billet is a small piece of paper upon which a person writes his or her name, birthdate, etc. Some psychics hold it, using psychometry to tune into the person throughout a psychic reading. I have known psychics to keep these at the end of a reading, especially if it were someone the psychic felt drawn to (usually sexually). They then use it to project energy to the individual for several days. Then the psychic calls "innocently" and the individual is amazed at the coincidence, since the psychic has been on the individual's mind also. This opens the door for further manipulation.

Remember that most psychics are very honest and don't employ such tactics, but it does go on. We should be aware of this and make sure that we get our billets back.

---

[2] Charles W. Cosimo. *Psionics 101*. (St. Paul, MN: Llewellyn Publications, 1986), p. 82.

3. **Keep information and plans about yourself to yourself.**

There is strength in silence. If someone does not know your plans, then it becomes extremely difficult for that person to inappropriately interfere or affect them. I have seen people in this field try to inadvertently affect events of other professional workers. It always astounds me when this goes on—especially by people who should know better, but they always wonder why their life just becomes more and more troublesome and unhealthy.

4. **Never accept gifts or hospitality from someone you suspect.**

We are often taught as children to accept hospitality and good intentions from others. Sometimes we feel guilty if we don't respond in kind. If we suspect someone of playing psychic games, NEVER accept hospitality or gifts.

Gifts can be plants—something planted upon us or in our home to adversely affect us. Objects can be charged with a thought or contain something hidden meant to influence us inappropriately.

In the old movies about vampires, it was told that a vampire could not enter a person's home unless invited. The same process holds true in psychic attacks and manipulation.

Remember too that guilt is a wonderful manipulative toy. If we invite or accept the invitation of someone we suspect, we open the doors for him or her to continue. Refer to Chapter 4 for more information on manipulation.

5.   Avoid contact with the suspected party.

The less contact on any level, including phones and letters, the less trouble. Often phone calls and such are used to re-establish a stronger connection. Sometimes it is feasible and beneficial to change phone numbers and arrange for the number to be unlisted.

If by chance we do encounter the suspected individual in public, keep conversations brief. Avoid eye contact, since the eyes are the gateway to the soul. Provide no information about your activities, even in idle conversation.

Preventing Psychic Attacks

True psychic attacks are rare. Prevention is always the best medicine for all aspects of health and well being.

As we will see in Part II, the key to protecting our energy is the human aura. The stronger and more vital it is, the less trouble and imbalance we will ever experience on any level. Sunlight strengthens the aura, along with conditioning for the physical body. Spending time in Nature is also tremendously beneficial to the auric field.

If we are working in the field or developing our abilities, we should close our psychic centers periodically. Many old time psychics believe that if they close down, they may not be able to open up again. If we developed our abilities properly, we should be able to close down and open up at will.

If we do experience difficulties, we should eat something every two hours or so. In this way our body's energies are focused on digestion and less open to other things. We should clean our bowels, and we should discontinue all occult practices, psychic development, and meditations. In meditation we become more passive, but we can substitute prayers for meditation, keeping our energies more electrical. If we do continue meditating, it should be on positive qualities and high ideals.

We should also clean the environment, physically and spiritually. The exercises in Part II will provide wonderful and enjoyable ways of cleansing the environment psychically. Incorporate powerful invocations for this. The Banishing Ritual of the Pentagram exercise described in Chapter 11 is one of the most effective.

We can also involve ourselves in new activities, crafts, and hobbies. By keeping the mind and hands occupied, we are less susceptible to outside influences, or at the very least,

PREVENTING PSYCHIC ATTACKS

1. Keep your aura strengthened.

2. Remove yourself from the environment for a while.

3. Resist unwanted fantasies and thoughts.

4. Spend time in Nature.

5. Forgive yourself for the involvement.

6. At the first hint or suspicion, pay attention to your dreams.

7. Laughter will break bonds.

8. Bless the individual.

9. Sometimes an actual response is required.

10. In times of greatest need, there is an occult police.

recognize them less. In the case of genuine psychic attack, remember there are a number of things you can do to lessen the effects. I describe them briefly in the following paragraphs.

If there is an actual attack, remember that the individuals involved will expend much more energy trying to manipulate you than you will have to expend defending yourself. It will take a greater toll upon them more quickly. Serious health problems often manifest for those using their energy to manipulate or attack. So if there is an actual attack or manipulation, persistence in our defense and in daily balancing will be rewarded. The attackers will eventually desist, having to put their time and energy into the disruptions and health problems that will plague them from their inappropriate activities.

Keep the aura strengthened. The Middle Pillar exercise and other techniques found in Part II are best for this. The stronger the aura, the greater our defense, and the less likely we are to feel the effects of outside influences.

Although this is not always possible, remove yourself form the environment for a while. At least we can change our routine. The less predictable we are, the less trouble we will experience.

Resist unwanted fantasies and thoughts as these are often an indication of outside interference.

Spend time in Nature. Nature is the great healer. There are so many benefits from a walk in Nature that we can do a number of books on it. Walks in Nature strengthen the aura and keep us grounded.

Forgive yourself for the involvement. Do not give it more energy and more openings through self-blame and self-recrimination. We are humans and we are going to make mistakes. Self-blame, guilt, and recriminations makes us impotent.

At the first hint or suspicion, pay attention to your dreams. They offer wonderful ways of gaining insight into what is going on. Our subconscious mind misses nothing, but it sometimes has to communicate what it perceives through dreams.

Laughter will break bonds. Laughter truly is the best medicine and can be used to diffuse most situations.

Bless the individual. This is sometimes difficult, but someone who wants to hurt truly needs to be healed.

Sometimes an actual response is required. I have a personal attitude of: "I don't do such things to others, so I won't tolerate it being done to me." I will forgive and bless, but I also do not hesitate to defend strongly.

I know people who have been the focus of attack. In most cases, the ones doing the attacking rarely attack the intended party directly. They attack a weak spot—a child, a loved one, a family member. They attack the individual indirectly by attacking the home, family, and friends to weaken, distract, and harm.

In the beginning of this chapter there is a quote: *"Evil prospers when good people do nothing."* Those who attack the innocent are evil, especially when it is done deliberately to wound or hurt someone else. In such cases, there are appropriate and righteous responses. They are not covered in this book, as the techniques in Part II will cover 99 percent of all problems ever encountered. Remember though that at times, a more active response is necessary.

In times of greatest need, there is an occult police. When all else has failed, it may be necessary to call on the occult police. These are individuals who operate in the physical and etheric realms.

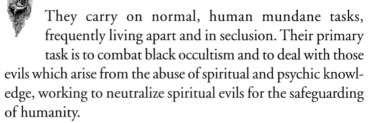

They carry on normal, human mundane tasks, frequently living apart and in seclusion. Their primary task is to combat black occultism and to deal with those evils which arise from the abuse of spiritual and psychic knowledge, working to neutralize spiritual evils for the safeguarding of humanity.

I first encountered this police in my situation with the group from Texas. It was through their timely intercedence that worst things did not occur. When all other avenues have been tried or in cases of grave emergency, they have a wonderful way of showing up without being asked. They are true Guardians.

If we genuinely wish to avoid difficulties and accelerate our spiritual growth, we must strive to become a spiritual warrior. To do so we must work toward purification. We must have dedication of character. We must be intellectually capable of strong fidelity to responsibility. We must become serene and express courage.

It has been said that we must wear the helmet of higher salvation and the breastplate of righteousness. We should wield the sword of spirit and truth and carry the shield of faith. We do not have to be perfect in these things, but by striving for them we open to wonders only imagined. We discover what is truly our divine right.

EGYPTIAN CHARM
This bronze magic hand, intended to avert the evil eye, is
covered with occult symbols: serpents with cock's comb, the pine
cone, the frong, and the winged caduceus.
(British Museum, London)

PART II:

Becoming the Spiritual Warrior

*Where the spirit does not work
with the hand, there is no art.*
Leonardo Da Vinci

Chapter 6

The Key to Protection

There is a vitality, a life force, an energy, a quickening,
that is translated through you into action, and
because there is only one of you in all time,
this expression is unique. And if you block it, it will
never exist through any other medium and will be lost.

Martha Graham

The key to protection is the vitality of the human aura. The aura is the energy field that surrounds the human body or anything with an atomic structure. Within the atoms that comprise all matter are electrons and protons—positive (electrical) and negative (magnetic) charges. The more animate the life and matter, the more vibrant the aura or energy field surrounding it.

We now have the technology available that can identify, measure, and verify the energy fields that surround the human body. Science has the capability of measuring how the human aura interacts with outside energy fields.

It is important to know how our auric field interacts with outside forces and energies and how our own aura interacts and affects the energies of others. The more aware we are of the human aura and its characteristics, the easier it is to determine when and how best to strengthen, balance, and cleanse our energy field. For our own well-being, we need to be sensitive when our aura weakens and loses energy.

With a strong and vibrant aura, those negative, draining, and unbalanced energies are deflected. There are many ways of vitalizing and strengthening the human aura. Maintaining a strong aura is not at all difficult. Positive health practices such as sunlight, fresh air, and physical exercise are extremely vitalizing to our auric field. Meditation can also be strengthening and protective. We will examine some of the best meditation exercises for the aura later in this chapter.

The Human Aura

The human aura forms elliptically around the human body and extends 8 to 10 feet in all directions with the average person. The healthier we are, physically and spiritually, the more vibrant and stronger our own auras will be, the more energy we will have, and the less likely we will be to come under outside influences.

Weak auras are more likely to be impinged upon by outside influences, affecting us physically, emotionally, mentally, and spiritually. Those with weak auras are more easily manipulated and tire more easily in most activities. From an emotional level, a weakened aura will generate feelings of being depressed, of being a failure, of not being in control of one's own life. In weakened auras, stresses reveal themselves more quickly.

THE HUMAN AURA

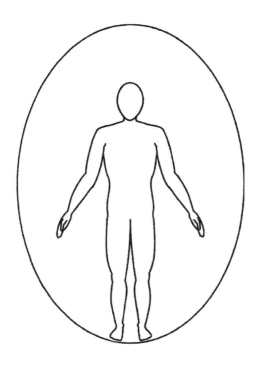

Part of the aura is comprised of our subtle body discussed earlier, but it is also comprised of energy emanations from the body. When the food we eat and the air we breathe is converted into energy by the cells of the body, the cells give off a byproduct called photon radiation (light emanations), which also comprise part of our auric field.

The human body has other energy emanations as well. The human body in its magnificence gives off light, sound, thermal energies, electricity, magnetic responses, heat, and more. Some of these energy fields are generated within the body and others are received from outside the body and then transformed by the body. This occurs through the natural interaction between one energy field and another, almost like a kind of osmosis between our personal energies and those energy fields around us.

The energies of Nature, for example, are easily absorbed and transformed by the body. A common prescription for recuperation after illness was to visit the ocean where the environment would help restore balance through the four elements: fire of the sun, water of the ocean, sand of the earth, and the air of the ocean breeze. The human aura would absorb these healing energies easily, strengthening and balancing the body.

Understanding the Aura's Role in Protection

We are constantly giving off (electrical) and absorbing (magnetic) energy through the aura. Because our aura is primarily electromagnetic, it has a great ability to interact with all other electromagnetic fields: plant, animal, mineral, and human. The more aware we are of this, the more we can use it to enhance our overall health and help prevent problems from arising.

Our aura can easily interact with the auras of other people, of plants, and of a multitude of other fields. If we are not aware of this potential exchange, we easily find ourselves drained at the end of the day. If we are around many people in the course of the day, we accumulate a lot of psychic energy debris. Think of it as an energy "static cling."

As a result, by the end of the day, we may have a multitude of strange thoughts and ideas running through our heads, and they may have nothing to do with our own levels of i nsanity. They have to do with what we picked up from all of those with whom we had interaction throughout the day. The more we are aware of it, the more we can prevent it.

Our aura also interacts with the energies of places, plants, and animals. Everything in nature has its own energy field and has the capability of interacting with our own. Tree, plant, and rock auras can be used to help us. We must study the qualities of these. We do not, within the course of this text, have the capability of understanding all of the intricacies of every plant, tree ,and stone, but we will examine some of the more beneficial ones in the chapter on protection through nature.

For example, if we have some aches and pains, we could go sit underneath a willow tree for a little while. The auras of willow trees are very soothing to aches and pains—particularly muscular aches. From an herbal aspect alone, willow trees are amazing; its bark contains a chemical called salicin which is the basic chemical used in aspirin. While sitting beneath a tree, our aura intermingles with that of the tree, stimulating a corresponding response in the body.

Pine trees and evergreens have wonderful auras for cleansing and balancing strong emotions, especially feelings of guilt. I have a wonderful old blue spruce tree in my front yard, and I can be found sitting under it a half hour before my family visits and for several hours afterwards.

By developing greater sensitivity to our energy field, we can monitor how it is responding and use tools to help keep it strong, whether through crystals, trees, or a variety of other techniques and tools.

Because of the electromagnetic aspects, we leave traces of our energy in places and on objects. The longer and more intimate the contact with a place or thing, the greater the energy imprint upon it. This is why pictures and personal items are links to us. In Dr. Karl Pribram's experiments at Stanford University, he concluded that the human brain and energy operates much like a hologram:

> A hologram is a special type of optical storage system that can be explained by an example: if you take the holographic photo of, say, a horse, and cut one section of it, e.g., the horse's head and then enlarge the section to the original size, you will get, not a big head, but a picture of the whole horse. In other words, each individual part of the picture contains the whole picture in condensed form. The part is in the whole and the whole is in each part...[1]

The key is that the part is a link to the whole. This is why we should be careful and control who has personal object of ours or access to them. Through the power of thought projection, a personal item (charged with our own auric energy) becomes a doorway or window directly to us. The part is a link to the whole.

---

[1] Wilbur, Ken, ed. *The Holographic Paradigm.* (Boulder, CO: New Science Library, 1982), p. 2.

PART II: BECOMING THE SPIRITUAL WARRIOR

Homes in which strong emotional events occurred are magnetized with the aura energies of the inhabitants. Individuals that are sensitive may feel uncomfortable in such environments and may even jump to the conclusion that the place is haunted. Most of the time, such experiences are merely the results of imprints that have not been cleansed. The methods described in the next chapter—particularly smudging techniques—will cleanse environments of imprinted traces of past residents and energies.

The basis of psychometry (attuning to the vibrations of an object) is a direct result of the magnetizing of the object by the owner's aura and its link to the owner, as explained through the holographic theory. By holding an object imprinted with the energy of the individual, a good psychic can tune into the individual.

The key to successfully protecting all of our energies lies in the aura. No psychic attack can take place unless the aura is weakened or pierced. Think of the aura as an electric fan. The healthier we are, the faster it spins. The less healthy we are, the slower it spins. Now think of a strip of paper, about 1 inch by 12 inches, as an outside force. If we were to hold one end of the paper and then try to slide the strip of paper through a fan's fast spinning blades, we would be unsuccessful. The breeze created by the blades would either blow the strip back away or the blades would chew it up, not allowing the paper to affect its speed. If our fan (our aura) is on high, the strip of paper (outside forces) can not enter into the blades.

The slower the fan blades spin, the easier it is to slip the paper into the fan and through the blades. The more vibrant and strong our aura, the less likely we are to have anything slip into and gum up our works. A healthy aura, because of its high vibrational rate, prevents the approach of non-material entities and energies without our permission—whether we are awake or asleep. Our aura is like a fan which, while on high, blows the paper back away.

A strong aura can also provide protection against physical harm. There is a vibrancy and confidence about it that is subtly picked up by those around who may think of doing harm. Individuals such as muggers look for victims who seem to be timid and carry themselves in a less assertive posture. If our aura is strong, it will reflect the kind of energy that is less tempting to muggers, and it will reflect back negative energies that otherwise might intrude.

The principle of resonance also applies here. Resonance is the ability of a vibration to reach out and trigger a response in something of like nature. If there is nothing that negative energies, thoughts and other projections can respond to or resonate within us, they pass by. With strong auras, negative and destructive atmospheres are deflected, as are mundane influences as well.

Remember that atmospheres are usually created by the human mind and so control begins with our own mind—our own self-control and preventive measures. Control of the environment begins with control of the aura. Nothing is more essential to control and strengthening of the aura than our own physical health.

Our greatest preventive tool is our physical health. With physical health and a vibrant aura comes opportunity to open new doors and awaken to new wonders without being overwhelmed or unbalanced in the process. In that way our spiritual search and our psychic development remains productive, enjoyable, and beneficial. Then, if something untoward happens, we can draw upon other more esoteric tools.

The exercises in this chapter are ones that are dynamically preventive of problems since they will strengthen the aura

WEAK VS. STRONG AURAS

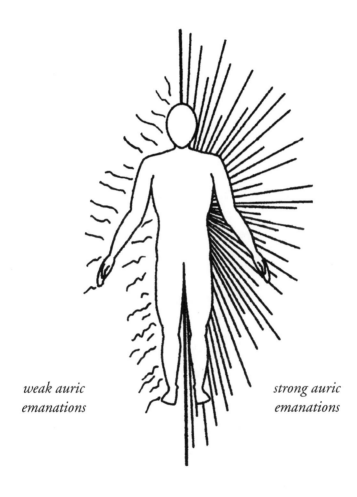

*weak auric
emanations*

*strong auric
emanations*

WHAT WEAKENS THE AURA

- poor diet
- lack of exercise
- lack of fresh air
- lack of rest
- stress
- alcohol and drugs
- smoking
- emotional upheavals
- fear and worry
- guilt and blame
- negative habits
- improper psychic activity

and enhance overall health. They, or some variation of them, should be a part of our daily health regimen and by doing them regularly, we will find ourselves more creative and productive in all we do.

The Empathic Aura

One of the most heightened forms of psychic sensitivity is empathy, which is often considered one of the most ancient of the healing arts. History is filled with legends and myths of individuals who took upon their own shoulders the aches, pains ,and sins of others. Most people have heard tales or stories of individuals who, by touching another's ache or pain, healed it. If we examine folklore around the world, we can find stories of those who could see through the eyes of others (including the eyes of animals). There are even tales of individuals who, by touching another person, are able to draw the illness into their own body and then transmute it there.

Everyone is empathic at some point. Most usually don't realize it when it occurs. Some people are empathic all of their life, and not understanding what is occurring, assume that something is wrong with them.

Life conditions, physiological changes, and psychic development can heighten our natural sensitivities. When we are more empathic, the aura is more magnetic, and outside forces and energies register upon us much more strongly and intensely than normally. Our body becomes the barometer for all that we are experiencing. Physical feelings, emotions, and mental attitudes can register so strongly upon us that we assume they are our feelings—when what we are feeling may actually be tied to someone we encountered, the location we are at, or a number of other possibilities. Energies outside of us register upon our aura so strongly and intimately that we feel they are our own.

For those involved in psychic development and healing work, it is important to recognize this natural tendency since it is very easy to link with the problems and issues of others and then to carry them with us as if they are our own. If we are not aware of this tendency, we can begin to think we are going crazy.

The following page has some questions to ask ourselves to help determine if we are empathic. If we answer "yes" to more than two, if might be a good idea to learn more about empathy and to use some of the aura strengthening and cleansing techniques daily.

Remember that because of the electromagnetic aspects of the aura, we are constantly exchanging energies with others and picking up energies imprinted on places. We must constantly be watchful and monitor what we feel in response to all stimuli, which is difficult, but our sanity and health requires it at times.

If you have a strong tendency to be empathic, there are several things that can be done. First, take time at the end of the day, visualizing yourself in some way disconnecting with everyone with whom you have had an encounter. By doing so, we are able to discern more easily whether what we are feeling is truly our own feelings or what we have picked up from others we have met. Even disconnect from family and loved ones. We will reconnect again, but if we are empathic, we need to have some time every day in which we are not linked to others at all. Doing so enables us to be more objective.

We can also use aromatherapy to help us with this tendency. We will explore this more in the next chapter, but if we do have empathic tendencies, we should always have on stock two essential oils—gardenia and eucalyptus.

ARE YOU EMPHATHIC?

- Are you easily influenced or persuaded by others to participate in things you normally would not? (including purchasing things you wouldn't normally buy.)

- Are you or were you shy and introverted?

- Do you go through mood swings, according to the group you are with?

- Do you find yourself quickly and easily tired or drained in social situations?

- Do you seem to always know what others are feeling or thinking?

- Do you have a way with animals?

- Have you ever felt others watching you without actually seeing them?

- Are you a touchy-feely kind of person?

- Does it make you uncomfortable to be touchy-feely with others?

- Can you tell if something of yours is out of place before actually seeing or discovering it?

- Do you find it difficult to determine what you are truly feeling at any particular time?

- Do you find it difficult separating home and work?

- Do you have difficulty seeing people and situations objectively?

- Are you over-emotional or hypersensitive, taking everything more personally and seriously than others?

- Do you have a tendency to take on everyone else's problems, aches, pains, worries, and battles?

Gardenia oil helps us to remain objective while dealing with others. It strengthens the aura, and it helps prevent us from being drawn into others' problems. Over the years I have recommended it countless times to professional healers, social workers, and psychics.

Eucalyptus oil should also be in everyone's medicine chest, particularly if we have a tendency to empathy. By using eucalyptus oil, we can help to diminish erratic emotional responses, taking the edge off and softening the emotional intensities. Although we still experience the emotions, they are in a much more controlled state.

EXERCISE: The Middle Pillar of Light

BENEFITS:

- strengthens the aura
- increases energy and vitality
- calms and balances, healing

The Middle Pillar of Light exercise[2] is taken from the ancient mystical Qabala, a spiritual map known as The Tree of Life that reflects the energies and forces found within the universe and correspondingly within the essence of every human being. The Tree of Life is comprised of three pillars or columns of light upon which are located ten spheres known as temples. In these temples the universal forces and our own consciousness intersect. The pillars are the primary channels for the flow of both universal forces and our own creative energies through our life and us.

The central or middle pillar is the balancing pillar and runs the median of the body, harmonizing opposing forces—

---

[2] This exercise is available on audio cassette and can be attained through your local store. For more information, see pages 356-357.

EXERCISE:

masculine and feminine, electrical and magnetic, yin and yang, ida and pingala. The middle pillar is the channel, which balances and strengthens the powerful forces and potentials within us, manifesting them into our essence and our life more tangibly, permanently, and consciously.

This exercise employs sound (ancient Hebrew names for the Divine), visualization, and breathing by using the ancient Hebrew names for God like mantras in conjunction with specific images and breathing rhythms. We can pump tremendous amounts of energy into the human aura, helping to seal leaks and to balance and heal, increasing our energy levels so that we have greater amounts with which to accomplish our tasks, helping to prevent us from being drained.

This exercise is one of the first that I ever teach developmental groups. It is a part of my own daily regimen, and I perform it before and after every workshop or seminar which I present. I recommend it as part of everyone's daily regimen.

Some people get hung up on the pronunciation of the Hebrew names. Yes, correct pronunciation is important, but not as important as intention and focus. The names are spelled out phonetically. For those wishing a more specific and correct pronunciation, this exercise and the Banishing Ritual exercise described in Chapter 12 can be found on my audio-cassette, *Psychic Protection*. More information on this and other related cassettes can be found in the back of this book.

PREPARATIONS

Make sure that you will not be disturbed for this exercise. Disconnect the phone, and inform others in your home

The Middle Pillar of Light

THE TREE OF LIFE

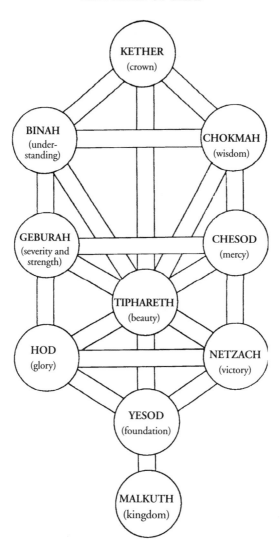

EXERCISE:

THE TREE OF LIFE
WITHIN THE HUMAN AURA

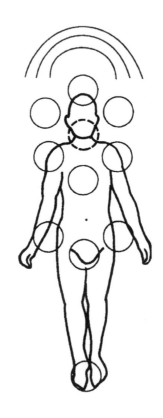

The Middle Pillar of Light

that you need some time alone. You may wish to light incense or use an essential oil that is strengthening and cleansing. Frankincense, cedar, sage, and sandalwood are good for this.

Make yourself comfortable. Take a seated position, feet flat on floor and back straight. Take a few deep, slow breaths and allow yourself to relax. Allow your eyes to close and breathe deeply.

THE MEDITATION

1. **Imagine and visualize a stream of light descending out of the heavens from a distant star.**

   It gathers just above the crown of your head, a soft pulsating crystalline light. It is vibrant and alive with energy. And as you vibrate the divine name, that light grows brighter and stronger, awakening and strengthening the crown center.

2. **Slowly sound the divine name of Eheieh (ay-huh-yay).**

   Inhale deeply, sounding the name silently. As you exhale, sound it out audibly. Emphasize each syllable, drawing it out. Feel the crown of your head coming alive. Repeat this name 5-10 times. The toning of the name should correspond to your breathing. Inhale, sounding it silently. Exhale, sounding it audibly.

EXERCISE:

3. **From that sphere of light, a shaft descends to the area of the throat where a second sphere of light begins to form.**

    Visualize this second sphere of light illuminating and energizing the throat area of the body. With each repetition of the Divine name, this center grows more alive and strong within you. You now have a shaft of light that descends out of the heavens to the crown of your head and down to the throat area of the body.

4. **Sound forth the Divine name for the second sphere, Yehovah Elohim (yah-hoh-vah-ay-loh-heem).**

    Repeat this name 5-10 times, feeling and seeing this second sphere of crystalline energy come to life within you.

5. **From this second sphere, the shaft of light descends down to the area of the solar plexus. There a third sphere of light forms. With each repetition of the Divine name, Yehovah Aloah va Daath (yah-hoh-vah-ay-loh-ah-vuh-dahth), this sphere grows stronger and more vibrant within you.**

    Repeat this Divine name 5-10 times, feeling the sphere and its energy grow stronger. You have now created a third sphere of light, linked to the other two and the heavens by a brilliant shaft.

6. **From this third sphere, the shaft descends to the area of the base of the spine. There a fourth sphere of light begins to form. With each repetition of the Divine name, Shaddai El Chai (shah-dye-ehl-heye), the fourth sphere grows stronger and more vibrant within you.**

The Middle Pillar of Light

Repeat the Divine name 5-10 times, feeling the entire base of the spine growing stronger and more vibrant. Remember to coordinate the toning of the name with the breathing. You have now awakened this fourth sphere and linked it to the other three with a brilliant shaft of light running through you.

7. **From this fourth sphere of light, the shaft descends down to the arches of the feet. There a fifth sphere of light gathers, and the shaft continues into the heart of the earth.**

   You now have a pillar of light extending from the heavens down through your body and into the heart of the earth.

   Five spheres of light are formed within you, and with each repetition of the Divine name, Adonai ha Aretz (ah-doh-neye-hah-ah-retz) the fifth sphere comes alive strong within you.

   Repeat this name five to ten times, feeling the fifth center coming alive within you. You have now formed the living pillar of light through your aura and your entire body.

8. **Bring your attention back to the crown of the head and begin slow rhythmic breathing.**

   With each outbreath, light and energy streams down that shaft from the heavens through the sphere at the crown of your head and down the left side of your body. As you inhale, the energy is drawn up the right side. Repeat this 5-10 times feeling the aura extending and strengthening above and beside you.

EXERCISE: The Middle Pillar of Light

9. **Now, as you continue rhythmic breathing, the direction of that stream of light changes.**

   As you exhale the light streams down the front of the body, and as you inhale, you draw it up the back. Repeat this 5-10 times. Visualize your aura growing stronger and more vibrant. With these two breaths, your aura is enlarged, pumped full of new energy.

10. **Visualize rainbow energy rising up that shaft out of the earth through you as the pillar of light, and then spraying out the crown of the head to fill your aura with rainbow hues.**

    Coordinate the rhythmic breathing with this. As you inhale, you draw the energy up through you, and as you exhale you spray it out the crown of the head to fill your aura with rainbow light of healing and balance.

With this exercise you become a living pillar of light. Take a few moments at the end to feel your aura vibrant all around you. Take a few slow deep breaths, allow your eyes to open, and resume your daily activities.

EXERCISE: The Ida-Pingala Exercise

> ### BENEFITS:
> - balancing
> - a quick energizer
> - temporarily restores lost energy

This exercise is a yoga breathing technique, sometimes called *alternate nostril breathing,* and is wonderfully effective for a quick fix when our energy drops or is suddenly drained.

Fresh air and proper breathing is essential to the vibrancy and strength of the aura. Nostril breathing, rather than mouth breathing, is the correct manner to energize our entire system. Mouth breathing makes us more susceptible to health problems because we do not have the sinuses to warm the air or nostril hairs to help filter it. Mouth breathing does not always help the vitality of the aura.

In yoga, there is breathing that balances the male and female, the electric and magnetic. When both aspects are balanced, we are healed and strengthened. This is called *susumna.* Combining a moon breath (magnetic or ida) with a sun breath (electric or pingala), we quickly energize the aura

EXERCISE:

and balance out our electromagnetic aspects. This exercise also enhances memory. I often recommend it to individuals before studying since it will help us learn the material more quickly and retain it longer.

The technique is comprised of alternate nostril breathing. Inhaling through one nostril, holding the breath and then exhaling out the opposite. Using the thumb and fingers to close and open the nostrils is easiest for most people. This exercise is also greatly enhanced by performing it outdoors in the fresh air.

1. **Begin with a slow exhale and place the tongue at the roof of the mouth behind the front teeth.**

   This tongue positions helps to link energy pathways or meridians—governing and conception—enhancing the energizing effects of this breathing technique.

2. **Using your thumb, close the right nostril and inhale slowly through the left nostril for a count of four.**

3. **Keeping the right nostril closed, use your fingers to close down the left nostril so that both nostrils are closed for a count of eight.**

4. **Keeping your left nostril closed, remove your thumb from the right nostril, and exhale out of it for a slow count of four.**

The Ida-Pingala Exercise

5. **Then switch. Close down the left nostril and inhale slowly for a count of four through the right.**

6. **Close the right nostril and with both nostrils closed, hold for a count of eight.**

7. **Keeping the right nostril closed, slowly exhale for a count of four out the left nostril.**

8. **Repeat this four to five times, inhaling and exhaling through each nostril.**

   Breathe in one, hold and exhale out the other. Reverse and repeat the procedure. This will saturate your aura and your body with quick energy.

   When finished, move slowly, for there may be some initial dizziness. If so, it will pass quickly. The energy will build over the following few minutes before it stabilizes.

Exercise: The Cleansing White Fire Vortex

> ### Benefits:
> * purifying
> * excellent preparation for psychic work
> * quick cleansing for post-group situations
> * aids the disconnecting from empathic responses

This is a wonderful exercise for cleansing the aura, especially in preparation for psychic work or after. It is also beneficial when we need to cleanse and ground ourselves after exposure to group situations. Use this exercise at the end of a day or after having interacted with a great many people. It combines visualization and breathing, and it only takes about 15 minutes.

This exercise has two phases. One is the pyramid cleansing and the other is the cleansing vortex. It can be performed without the triangulation or pyramid phase, but the pyramid helps to loosen up the debris, especially in conjunction with the chakras.

1. **Begin by visualizing a crystalline ball of light about 12 inches above the crown of the head.**

   As you focus on the ball of light, exhale and it begins to move downward and in front of you at an angle about 12 inches in front of the brow. As you inhale, this sphere of light is drawn into the brow.

   As it enters into the brow, it cleanses and purifies the brow center and moves to the back of the head. As you exhale, it rises up the back of the head through the crown (cleansing it), and it returns to its original point above the head.

PYRAMID CLEANSING

EXERCISE:

2. **Repeat this with the throat, heart, solar plexus, spleen, base, knees, and arches of the feet. (Refer to the diagram on the following page.)**

    With each breath the original sphere cleans and loosens the debris in each chakra and helps clean the channel of energy up the spine.

    As you exhale, the sphere moves down to the front of the body to a position outside and in front of the chakra. As you inhale, it is drawn into the chakra, cleaning and purifying it. As you exhale, the sphere rises up along the spine to its original point above the head.

3. **The last pyramid cleansing is to a point below the feet about 12 inches into the earth.**

    This time when the sphere enters, the sphere clones itself, sending one aspect into the heart of the earth, while the other rises up through the body. Visualize it as a small boring light, loosening and cleansing an energy pathway through you and linking you to the earth and the heavens.

4. **Now visualize a cleansing vortex descending upon you.**

    About 30 feet above you, visualize a small tornado or whirlwind of crystalline white fire energy beginning to form. It is in fact a small spiritual tornado.

    As it forms its funnel shape and descends, see it encompassing your entire auric field. The small end of the funnel enters into the crown of your head and slowly the vortex descends through your body, burning off all of the energy debris loosened through the pyramid cleansing.

The Cleansing White Fire Vortex

5. **As this spiritual vortex moves through your body, it descends into the earth itself.**

   Visualize this vortex as carrying all of your energy debris and contaminates into the lower realms where it is used to fertilize and benefit lower kingdoms of life upon and within the planet. See yourself as purified and cleansed, with your energy flowing free without any obstructions.

THE WHITE FIRE VORTEX

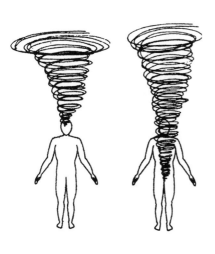

EXERCISE: 𝕿𝖍𝖊 𝕻𝖔𝖘𝖙𝖚𝖗𝖊 𝖔𝖋 𝕻𝖗𝖔𝖙𝖊𝖈𝖙𝖎𝖔𝖓

BENEFITS:
- prevents being drained
- closes aura from intrusion
- balances and calms
- prevents influence of others while in their presence

Earlier I spoke of problems that we all experience when we are around individuals who drain us. It is our energy though, and no one has the right to take it without our permission and without our knowledge. Even if the individuals are unaware that they do this, it is important that we be aware it is going on.

We have natural energy pathways within our body. In the Chinese tradition, these energy pathways are known as meridians, and they are closely connected to the nerve pathways of the autonomic nervous system. Our life force circulates in and around our body and its aura through the aid of the meridians.

These meridians have electrical and magnetic aspects. We can learn to direct our energies and close our circuit of energy so that our energies only circulate within our aura and doesn't

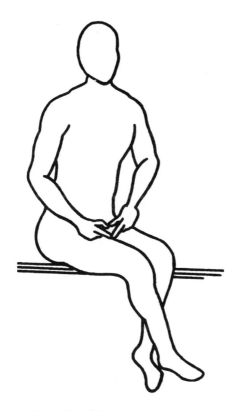

The Closed Circuit Posture

EXERCISE:

intermingle with others. Two points on the body are effective for this, and when utilized, they prevent others from draining us or sapping us of our energy.

One way of doing this is just by bringing the tips of the thumbs and fingers of both hands together. Most of our meridians terminate at the fingertips. By bringing the tips of both hands together, we close the circuit.

Actually, all that really needs to be done is to link the thumb and index fingers of both hands. If you are sitting in front of someone with the thumb and index fingers touching, the person may think you are putting a mojo or something on them, and although there are people I wouldn't mind thinking that, by just bringing all of the fingertips of both hands together upon our lap, it is a more natural posture.

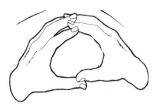

Hand Position

The Posture of Protection

To further emphasize this, cross the feet at the ankles. Between the closing of the circuit at one end (fingertips) and at the other end with the ankles(since most people cannot sit with the tips of their toes touching), we create a closed circuit. Our energy only circulates within our own field and not within that of others.

The next time you encounter someone who usually drains you, assume this posture. Rest your hands casually upon your lap, touch the fingertips together and cross the feet at the ankles. It is simple and casual, and no one will suspect a thing.

Over time you will get feedback. Even though the other party may not know what is going on, he or she will feel the difference. You may still be talking to them in the same way as always, you are just not allowing them to take your energy.

Part II: Becoming the Spiritual Warrior

Chapter 7

Simple Tools of Protection

*Every blade of grass has its Angel that bends over it
and whispers, "Grow, grow."*

The Talmud

At some point we realize that we are made of more than just the physical body. We begin to understandthat there is more to the world and to our essence than meets the eyes. Most people focus upon things that are only visible and tangible, but science demonstrates daily that many things not visible or tangible in the traditional sense affect us.

We know that fragrances, images, sounds, and music can affect us—physically, emotionally, mentally, and spiritually. If we are not aware of how extraneous forces can affect us, we can easily end up with weaknesses and imbalances within our energy systems. These may manifest as physical illnesses or as emotional or mental imbalances. Our energy systems are impinged upon everyday, and unless we learn to recognize these phenomena, we are more likely to experience unwanted intrusions and complications.

We have all had experiences in which our energies were affected by outside forces, such as extraneous sounds, heat, lights, or electrical frequencies. The more we realize this, the more we can use simple but effective tools to prevent this impinging.

In more ancient times, these simple tools would have been thought of as charms, spells, and the works of magic. What was once considered supernatural has today been proven to be scientifically natural. We can use the tools that were once considered magical to effectively strengthen and protect

Preparing a Charm

ourselves. Today we have the knowledge and understanding of how these "charms" actually work, and we will examine seven of the most common and effective tools of balance and protection we will ever need.

Seven Tools of Protection

We live in a society that holds great fascination for relics and charms of various sorts. These can be the wearing of a crucifix, the praying of a rosary, the lighting of a candle, the use of incense and even a gris gris bag.[1] If we believe they provide protection, then they will do so—to some degree. If wearing a charm or performing a particular ritual (no matter how superstitious) comforts us, we will be more relaxed psychologically and less influenced by outside circumstances. We will be healthier for it in the same way a child is comforted and sleeps better with his or her favorite blanket or stuffed toy.

The problem most people run into is sole reliance upon a single charm, prayer, or activity without the knowledge of what it is truly for or how to use it. How often have we heard prayers spoken in church that are rote, dry, and unempowered? We have all experienced a teacher or lecturer who was dry and put the audience to sleep. Do we assume that the divine forces in the universe, however we define them, will respond to our prayers and acts—no matter how dry and unimpassioned?

We need to understand how energy and its principles affect us so that we can work with it, keeping ourselves strong and vibrant. This involves learning to use a variety of tools and methods, according to the task at hand. Tools make our tasks more easily accomplished. They help us to stabilize ourselves as we develop our potentials more fully.

---

[1] A gris bag contains various items that serve as a magical charm for protection, love, or a variety of other purposes.

SEVEN TOOLS

FOR PROTECTION

1. Knowledge and
   Proper Intention

2. Healing Colors and
   Power Candles

3. Aromatherapy

4. Flower Elixirs

5. Prayer Shields and
   Mandalas

6. Forces of Nature

7. Ritual and Ceremony

An electrician must learn the basic principles of electricity and how to use the tools of his trade to correct problems and make repairs safely and effectively. The same idea presides in the spiritual and psychic world. Certain principles must be understood and certain tools developed, especially for those who intend or are already working within the psychic and spiritual field.

These following basic tools can be used by anyone to enhance their life. Each has its benefits individually and in combination with the others. All of these tools we will discuss throughout Part II in greater detail, but it is good to know something about all of them and how they work.

To some, these tools will seem like nothing more than magic and spell work. They are anything but that. They are tools based upon natural laws and principles of energy. Some are linked directly to holistic healing modalities.

1. Knowledge and Proper Intention

The more knowledge we have, the less likely we are to ever run into problems. Knowledge eliminates fear and promotes awareness of our highest and strongest capabilities. Through knowledge we not only learn to recognize subtle influences, but also how to prevent ourselves from being affected by those which may be detrimental or disruptive—physically or spiritually.

Just as through knowledge we can learn to care for our physical body more effectively, we can also use knowledge to help us care for our psychic and spiritual aspects as well. Knowledge enables us to strengthen our energies, enhance our abilities and prevent problems and complications from arising.

An old occult axiom states, "All energy follows thought." Where we put our thoughts is where our energy goes. By what we think and believe, by what we intend, we create the conditions for manifestation. Some people believe that they will catch two colds every winter, and thus as winter approaches, the body responds to that idea, making the individual more susceptible to "catch" those two colds. We create self-fulfilling prophecies.

In the Qabala, there operates an aspect of the Divine known as *Jehovah Aloah va Daath*—God made manifest in the sphere of the mind. The mind is at the heart of all that manifests within our life. Learning to use proper intention with proper knowledge will keep us protected in all situations. It eliminates fear and awakens our creative potentials. Used together, proper knowledge and intention can create better health and balance for the body, mind, and spirit.

2. Healing Colors and Power Candles

Color is a property of light. Every color has its own absorptive and reflective properties. Different frequencies of light (the various colors) will affect different human energies. Some play dynamically on the physical body and the functions of various bodily systems. Some affect emotional and mental states. Some affect the higher frequencies of the brain, stimulating spiritual and psychic perceptions.

Remember we are an energy system, as we discussed in the previous chapter. Energy vibration exists in all things. Because of this, we can use outside tools such as colors to interact with our own physical vibrations to heal a condition of the body, to create harmony within our environment, to awaken our psyche, and to strengthen our spirituality.

Candles are a magnificent tool for using light in all aspects of our life. There are many meditations, techniques, and exercises for using colors—especially in the form of candles—to strengthen the body, mind, and spirit. Just as the human body needs to stretch and exercise for better health and well being, the psyche needs to stretch and exercise as well. This doesn't mean we must learn contorted postures or lead a cloistered, monk-like existence. Candles are a very pleasant tool for augmenting our energies and for a variety of other purposes.

Candle meditations and exercises alleviate stress, awakening psychic sensitivity, while instilling balance. Less stress makes for better health. When we are calm and healthy, we are less susceptible to unwanted influences, be they pushy salespeople, irritating coworkers, negative thoughts, or unwanted psychic phenomena.

3. Aromatherapy

The study of fragrances and the use of aromatherapy in healing have grown in popularity in our modern world, and yet humans for a multitude of purposes have used fragrances in all traditions. They are some of the most beautiful and effective means of changing vibrations: physical, emotional, mental, and spiritual.

Oils and incenses can be used to counteract dis-ease and illness, to strengthen the aura; and to elevate the spirit and awaken our intuitive faculty. Fragrances can be employed as a tool to assist us in almost every aspect of our life.

Fragrance is a vibrational force we can use to interact with our aura, our bodies, and our environment. There are powerful fragrances and simple techniques anyone can use with just a basic knowledge to heal, balance, and protect. Some of the more protective fragrances and techniques for using them will be examined in greater detail later in this chapter.

4. Flower Elixirs

Flower elixirs are a form of modern "energy medicines" created from the energy patterns of flowers and trees. Used in holistic healing and psychological counseling, they operate in a fashion similar to homeopathic medicines.

There are as many uses for flower elixirs as there are flowers. Each flower has its own personality and thus its own vibrational energy with a unique effect. Flowers can be used to interact with our physical and spiritual energies for a wide variety of functions—from overcoming fears to perceiving nature spirits.

5. Prayer Shields and Mandalas

Prayer shields and mandalas have been used in many traditions upon the planet. They were used to mark off sacred space, to protect and to help open to spiritual forces. We live in a time in which science has demonstrated that geometry affects electromagnetic patterns—amplifying, diminishing, and even negating the frequencies of environments.

Shields and mandalas can be created to induce altered states of consciousness, to stimulate peaceful sleep, and to cleanse and purify environments. Some believe they are merely a psychological sugar pill, a placebo, but we know that all energy follows thought. We also know there is more going on with shields and mandalas than a placebo effect, even if we don't understand it all at this time. Most of us don't understand how electricity works, but it doesn't stop us from using it for our benefit.

6. Forces of Nature

Nature is one the most powerful resources we have. It contains forces and elements that we can use daily to heal, balance, strengthen, and bless ourselves. Every aspect of Nature has something we can use daily to enhance our lives. From the air we breathe to the fragrances of flowers and trees.

Animals, trees, flowers, and all of the elements of Nature can be used to strengthen and ground us when life seems to be getting away from us. There are so many ways, in fact, of working with Nature that an entire book could be written just on its healing capabilities. From herbs to totems, in Chapter 8 we will examine some of the more common and most effective ways Nature can protect us and strengthen us as we grow.

7. Ritual and Ceremony

There are many rituals and ceremonies for protection, healing, and balance. They incorporate many of the tools described above, combining them to elicit a much stronger impact. Although this book will not cover the entire realm of ritual, it will provide some advanced techniques for cleansing, healing, and protection that will help us in every area of our life.

From the chanting and praying of sacred words to the ceremonial use of fragrance, there are ways of creating ceremonies that are dynamically purifying and protecting. One such exercise in particular, taken from the ancient Qabala, is called the "Banishing Ritual of the Pentagram" and it will be provided in Chapter 11.

Some Useful Tools for Protection

The tools discussed throughout this book are simply tools. We each must find our own ways of working with them. The more we utilize them, the greater their ability to keep our energies vibrant and strong. The stronger we are, the less likely we are to be affected by outside influences—including other people.

The tools described in the following pages of this chapter are the ones most commonly used. They are the simplest and most enjoyable to work with, even helping correct more complicated problems if and when they arrive. These tools can be used effectively as part of our routine daily preventive care regimen. They are powerfully effective in combination with any technique throughout this book for physical health and psychic protection.

TOOL: **Healing Colors and Power Candles**

Often, when people think of psychic protection, they think of charms, amulets, and talismans or of people burning candles to weave spells. More often than not they do not know the difference between these tools or if they truly work.

Quantum physics has done much to explain the phenomena of psychic energy and many of the mystical tools of various traditions. Because we are energy operating on many levels, we have a wonderful ability to affect and be affected by extraneous forces. For this reason, we can use color and candles as a magnificent tool.

Colors can be used to help us concentrate, attune psychically, heal, and protect. Every color has its own unique quality that can affect us physically, emotionally, mentally and spiritually. Using them in the form of candles can be a powerful way of helping to protect and balance us.

The candle is a powerful symbol of activating fire within our life. The color of the candle and its vibrational frequencies are activated, released, and amplified when the candle is lit. As the candle burns, its color frequency (energy) is released into the environment and into our aura.

One of the most effective ways of using the candle is in meditation. Light the candle and sit in front of it. Breathe deeply, allowing yourself to relax. With each breath, feel yourself drawing in the color, filling your body and your aura with its frequency. See and feel the color filling the environment around you to heal, balance, bless, and protect.

Candles for Balancing and Protection

All colors have beneficial qualities although some colors are more effective for balancing and protection than others. By studying the significance of colors and their qualities, we can discern which color will be most effective for our own individual situation. Several good sources for information on colors can be found in the bibliography. If unsure which color to use, try any one of the five listed here.

BLACK

Many people fear the black candle. It has gotten a bad reputation in modern times because of movie and TV associations with things that are evil. Black is not an absence of light; it is like white and has all the colors of the rainbow within it.

Black candles are very grounding. They can help bring us back down to earth. In meditation it can help us to find the light within the dark. Meditating with a black candle can also help us to uncover secrets around us, especially in regards to things personally affecting us.

The black candle is one of the most protective we can use, stabilizing energies around us so they are less erratic. Burning a black candle also strengthens the aura, pulling it back closer around the body so it is less likely to be impinged upon.

Black candles work best when burnt with white candles, just as white candles work best with black. Together they balance and seal. They stabilize the aura and the energies operating around us—be they projections from others, unsettling thoughtforms, or spirit phenomena.

BROWN

Brown candles are also very grounding and stabilizing and can be good to burn somewhat regularly for those who have a tendency to be empathic. Burning a brown candle will help the empathic individual to discern more easily whether the feelings and impressions are one's own or those picked up from others.

Brown candles are effective when we are feeling spacey, helping to restore focus and eliminating a feeling of being scattered by stabilizing our mental and emotional states. Meditating with brown candles can stimulate a common-sense approach to problems and disruptions, helping to bring us "back down to earth" in our perspectives, increasing our discernment, and awakening greater certainty about issues that may be at the forefront.

RAINBOW HUES

Rainbow hues encompass seven colors: red, orange, yellow, green, blue, indigo, and violet. Together these colors will balance and help heal most major systems of the body.

In meditation, they awaken a sense of promise and a feeling that everything will be all right. Candles with rainbow hues can be used to follow up a protective candle meditation with any of the other colors listed here.

SILVER

Silver is a color that awakens a sense of new possibilities. In some ways, it operates like white in that it can amplify the effects of other colors.

In meditation, silver can be beneficial to help discover sources of troubles. It brings illumination and stimulates the intuition so that we can gain insight into illnesses, difficulties, and strange events—along with their sources.

If you feel that someone is projecting negative energies at you, meditate with a silver candle, asking for clarification. Within 24 hours, the answer will come. The individuals involved will initiate some physical contact, perhaps through a phone call, a visit, a letter, or some other way that is unusual or out of the blue. It is not unusual to have this occur within three hours of the meditation, often within 12 hours, but always within 24. If the troubles are just troubles of life and not projections of a particular person, events will continue as usual for the following 24 hours.

If unsure about whether the person who contacted you is truly projecting, repeat the meditation. If it is that person, he or she will contact you yet again within a short time after your meditation.

WHITE

Many people speak of "putting a white light around them," and it can be effective. White contains the whole color spectrum within it and thus using it can be a means of drawing upon and supplementing any colors or energies we need.

White is a traditional symbol of purity and power. A white candle will amplify the effects of other colors. For this reason, combining and burning a white candle with a black candle can be one of the most protective and balancing things we can do. Together they harmonize the polarities of the body and the atmosphere around us.

Quality white taper candles can be used to determine the presence of negativity around us. If it smokes a great deal and the smoke is dark, negativity is being burned off. As the smoke dissipates and the candle burns clean, it indicates the environment is clean as well. When the smoking ceases, the atmosphere around us has been cleansed.

Meditating with white candles will awaken hope and inspiration, stimulating new energy, healing, and opening up blocked movement in our life, especially if others are blocking it around us.

SACRED
CANDLE-LIGHTING
MEDITATION

As you strike the match, focus on it as a symbolic act. You are giving birth to a living flame. You are participating in the ritual of lighting fires that has been performed throughout the ages—from hearthstones of primitive man to the great solar fires of the stars.

This match is part of a single living flame, with its original spark in the heart of the Divine. The power of this act rests solely with the fires of your own imagination and spirituality.

As the fire is struck, remember that you are creating fire—causing light to shine where there was no light before. With this act, you bring warmth and change. This simple act brings healing to the soul for your are expressing the Divine within your environment. Your entire aura shines brighter, flaming strong.

As you take the flame to the candle, see the flame as the power of a great being or archangel or even the spirit of the Divine. It moves through space to bring light and life and new creation. Visualize the unlit candle as a dark planet or an unlit solar system or even an uncreated soul awaiting the touch of the Creator to bring its flame to life.

REMEMBER

Candle lighting should be a prelude
to your actual meditation, and the extinguishing
should be the last act of the meditation. This allows
all to return to rest and recuperation. Do not use the
breath to extinguish the flame for breath is also
creative. The creative should never be used
to extinguish something else that is creative.

TOOL: PROTECTION THROUGH AROMATHERAPY

Aromatherapy is one of the most effective means of changing, raising, or cleaning the vibrational frequencies of our aura or our environment. We do not have the capabilities of examining all of details of aromatherapy within this text, but there are some wonderful guides listed in the bibliography for those wishing to explore more fully the use and history of oils and incense.

Incense and fragrant oils have an ancient history in healing and ritual. Most of the early incenses and oils were made from bark, herbs, flowers, and other plants since each had its own characteristics. They are common tools for use in meditation and ritual. Each has its own unique effects and have been frequently used to alter the vibrational frequency of the aura and the immediate environment according to their unique characteristics. Some oils are antibacterial, while others elicit psychological responses.

Fragrances were used to mask bad odors and to pay homage to deities. Incense was a medium for prayer. As the smoke rose, so did the prayers and thoughts of the petitioner. Oils were used for anointing and blessing. Both have been used for healing and for communicating with spirits since some are more calming, and some are more stimulating. In every society, they have been used to counter the effects of dis-ease and negativity.

Smudging with Incenses

Incenses are commonly used in the form of joysticks and cones, usually for cleansing or changing the energy of the aura or the environment through smudging.

Smudging is a process to bless and purify a home, a person, or an environment. A smudge bundle, often herbs or incense, is lit. (The smudging process can also be done with a single joystick.) The lit bundle is breathed upon gently so that the smoke rises. With the hands or feathers, the smoke is brushed over and around the person or the home—especially doorways and windows to purify the area. Then the smudge bundle is often extinguished. If further meditation or ritual is to be carried out, the smudge bundle or joystick can also be left to burn itself out.

Care must be taken with smudge sticks and other types of incense to make sure they are not placed near anything flammable. There are many types of incense holders to help protect against fires. A good ceramic bowl with sand in it is most effective for smudge bundles (found at any new age or metaphysical store) or an appropriate holder to catch fallen ashes.

Working with Essential Oils

Essential oils are made through a distilling process, and they can be quite potent and intoxicating. There are many ways to use essential oils, but because of their potency, they are always best used in a diluted form.

Essential oils can be worn like a perfume, but they should always be diluted. Many essential oils are harsh and can burn or irritate the skin. They can also be massaged into the body. Many massage lotions contain essential oils. We can also bathe in them. With essential oils, a half a capful of oil per full tub of water is all that is needed. In this way the fragrance can touch the whole body, affecting us physically and spiritually, which in turn affects our aura as we wear the aroma and its beneficial effects upon us throughout the day or night.

To affect our environment, essential oils can be used in a variety of ways. A drop or two within a small bowl of water will allow its fragrance to fill a room. They can be used in vaporizers and potpourri pots to fill a room with a particular fragrance. There are also expensive diffusers on the market, which will put the fragrance out into the air for extended periods of time.

Incense and oils are beautiful tools that we can work with in a variety of ways. They lend themselves to individual adaptation. We can create our own personal anointing and blessing rituals by combining prayers, meditations, and various oils according to our purposes. Be creative in doing this. Trust your instincts.

Learning to use oils and incense can help us create an energy field around us that is strong and vibrant. We can use them to restore balance and health, to aid in protection, and to stimulate inner perceptions. The oils discussed in the following paragraphs are commonly available and used frequently for healing and blessing:

CARNATION

Carnation is one of the most ancient and most frequently used fragrances for healing and blessing. During medieval times, it was used to anoint the heads of the sick and dying. In Elizabethan England, it was worn to avoid an untimely death upon the scaffold.

Carnation is stimulating to the entire auric field and the body's metabolism. As it strengthens the aura, we are less likely to be impacted upon by outside energies and influences.

It can also be used to help clear the aura of negative thoughtforms.

CEDAR

Cedar is a cleansing and protection oil. In ancient Egypt it was believed to be imperishable with the ability preserve the human body. Solomon's temple was made entirely of cedar, and cedar was believed to have been used in the Temple of Diana at Ephesus. Cedar was a tree sacred to the unicorn, a fantastic creature and archetype of great strength, gentleness, and healing.

Cedar is soothing and strengthening, especially effective if our dreams are troubled. It is a good oil to use in the rooms of children and loved ones to protect them during sleep. Cedar makes a wonderful incense or oil to blend with others, as it will enhance the protectiveness and strength of other fragrances. It awakens hope, calming fears and worries, and is very cleansing to both the aura and environments.

EUCALYPTUS

As a dynamic healing oil, eucalyptus is one of three that I recommend be in everyone's medicine chest (the other two being gardenia and lavender). These three oils have healing and balancing capabilities that can be used for most of the health and emotional problems that which can arise around the home.

Eucalyptus helps breathing, is relaxing, and helps to ease both emotional and mental tensions. It is diminishing and calming to overly emotional states, and lowers the energy intensities to a bearable level. For several years of my teaching in the public school system, I worked at the junior high level where things are interesting because the kids are always changing from day-to-day. There were times when I knew I wouldn't be able to deal very well with their energy. On those days,

I would arrive earlier than usual and place a couple drops of eucalyptus oil into the heating register. The fragrance filled the room and lowered their energies a notch, making it more bearable for me. I saved it for special occasions when I needed a little less intensity.

Eucalyptus takes the edge off of emotional intensities and is effective to use if sleep is disturbed, especially by nightmares. It can be used to calm fears and worries, to strengthen the entire auric field, and to provide a nice boost to the immune system. It is powerfully effective to use throughout psychic development at night, so that newly awakened psychic energies are balanced in our sleep. It is also effective to use eucalyptus in homes where there are adolescence and prepubescent children or menopausal women to prevent the poltergeist type of phenomena from arising.

FRANKINCENSE

Frankincense is an ancient, sacred fragrance that has great application for healing and dynamic purification. It has been used to anoint the sick and for cleansing the aura. Meditating with it helps us gain insight on our obsessions and how best to break them. It can be used to awaken a stronger vision of health and, as a purifier, it is powerfully effective when used with the Banishing Ritual of the Pentagram exercise described in Chapter 11.

GARDENIA

Along with eucalyptus and lavender, gardenia is a wonderful oil that I recommend it be in everyone's medicine chest.[2] Gardenia can be used to prevent energy drains since it

---

[2] Lavender is not covered in this book. For more information on the healing properties of lavender, eucalyptus, and gardenia, refer to my earlier work, *The Healer's Manual* from Llewellyn Publications.

strengthens the aura to the degree that other people are less able to create strife and it stabilizes the aura around disruptive people and situations. It also helps repel negativity through the aura so the negativity does not get a chance to manifest in the physical body.

It has a very high spiritual vibration. I recommend gardenia oil to healers, social workers, counselors, psychics, or anyone dealing with a great number of people on emotional levels because it helps to prevent us from becoming emotionally attached to other people's problems. In this way, it is stabilizing for those working with emotionally disturbed people.

LEMON

Lemon is a wonderful cleansing fragrance. Old time mediums used it to clean their environments before seances and readings; its energy draws good spirits into the environment. This fragrance also stimulates clarity of thought. In psychic protection, this enables us to see the situation more clearly, rather than through fears and uncontrolled imaginings.

Lemon is a wonderful fragrance to use daily to eliminate stress since it relaxes the mind and the aura. In this way, the stress does not get a chance to weaken the aura and make us more susceptible to further problems.

ROSE

Rose is one of the most gentle, powerful, and spiritual fragrances and increase sthe effects of any healing modality. It can be used to balance and heal the chakras, thus strengthening the entire aura.

In psychic protection, rose awakens the ability to bless those who would try to disrupt or negatively influence us without making the link to us stronger. It also helps prevent others from tuning in and discovering what our activities are so they can attempt to disrupt them.

In mythology it was given to the God of Silence by Cupid to seal a promise not to reveal the love of Venus and Adonis. Because of this, it was used to wash the walls of banquet rooms in Rome so that whatever was said during the celebration would not be revealed outside the hall. It is a wonderful fragrance to insure our plans and activities remain secret and thus less able to be intruded upon—psychically or otherwise.

SAGE

Sage is one of the most powerful cleansing fragrances and is often the basis of Native American smudge bundles, frequently blended with cedar or sweetgrass. It is a wonderful tonic for cleansing and purifying under all circumstances.

Whether used as an oil or an incense, it relaxes and energizes the aura at the same time. Sage allows a freer flow of spiritual energy into the physical environment, while grounding and protecting the physical (body and environment) from imbalance, calming unbalanced psychic energies, and helping to free the body of stress and tension.

TOOL: FLOWER ELIXERS

Flower elixirs are a form of energy medicine, working in a similar manner to homeopathic medicines. Their development arose primarily out of the work of Dr. Edward Bach of England who explored and developed remedies in the plant world that would restore vitality. Bach's focus was finding plants for emotional and mental problems.

Using himself to test the effects, he developed 38 flower remedies that did not contain the physical material of the plants. Using a simple alchemical procedure, he extracted the energy behind and operating through the plant. The energy pattern is infused into a liquid. Each flower and plant has its own unique function and effect. A study of the flowers and their characteristics will assist us in determining the energy pattern.

Several companies in the United States now make elixers and distribute them. Most health food stores carry them or can direct you to them. The following companies are good sources:

The Dr. Bach Centre
Mt. Vernon, Sotwell
Wallingford, Oxon 0X10 OPZ
England

The Ellon Company
P.O. Box 320
Woodmere, NY 11598

The Flower Essence Society
P.O. Box 459
Nevada City, CA 95959

Flower remedies stimulate no physical discomfort, and they use only the pure and simple elements of Nature. They are benign and do not conflict with any other medication. The worse they can do is nothing.

There are a number of ways to use flower elixers. They can be taken internally so they work from the inside out, helping to restore balance physiologically. This in turn also balances the aura. Elixers can be used in baths or as a spritzer to give ourselves a boost. You can also spritz doorways and windows or other areas of the environment to cleanse, balance, and protect.

FLOWER REMEDIES AND THEIR BENEFITS

Flower	Energy
ANGELICA	opens us to the spiritual realms and angelic influences without becoming overwhelmed in the process
CENTAURY	for weakness of the will; awakens inner strength especially against outside pressures
CRAB APPLE	for feelings of uncleanliness and shame, especially when projected from outside; awakens harmony and inner cleansing
LAVENDER	excellent for psychic protection; soothing to nerves and to over-sensitivity to psychic development or psychic and spiritual experiences
OAK	awakens brave perseverance and strength; excellent for despair and despondency
OLIVE	excellent for mental and physical exhaustion; stimulates renewed vitality
PENNYROYAL	one of the most beneficial for psychic protection; cleanses aura; can be used in wash water to seal room or home; especially good in cases of psychic attack
PINE	calms over-emotional states; excellent for guilt and blame; eases fears and awakens positive self-confidence; cleansing to the aura

Flower Remedies and their Benefits (cont.)

Flower	Energy
RESCUE REMEDY	created from five Bach flower remedies, excellent for emergencies; balances, calms and stabilizes conditions; eases stresses, fears and worries
ROSE	helps awaken connection to angelic realm, allows only good spirits to influence, awakens love and spiritual inspiration
SAGE	helps control inner world experiences; healing, and strengthening to aura; cleansing to environment
SHASTA DAISY	spiritualizes the emotions and mind, allowing more objectivity when experiencing phenomena; assists in seeing entire picture; very effective in clarification when psychic attack or any manipulation is suspected
WALNUT	strengthening to aura, helps balance psychic energies during transitions (puberty, menopause, etc.) thus calming "poltergeist" activity; awakens objectivity and clear perspectives
WHITE CHESTNUT	excellent for unwanted thoughts, fears and worries; effective for any suspected manipulation; awakens quietness and clarity of mind
YARROW	especially good for psychic protection and for oversensitivity, strengthens the aura, awakens emotional clarity, eases stress

TOOL: THE POWER OF
SACRED SOUNDS

Sacred sound—through music, words, prayers, and chants—can be a powerful tool for healing and protection. The ability to use sound, music, and voice to create changes in others and us was at the heart of all the lost traditions. Every society had its teachings, religious and magical, in regards to how best to use sound, music, and voice.

We can not hope to cover the spectrum of applications of sacred sound and music to affect changes, but we can explore some of the more significant and effective ways to use sound and music for protection.[3] For the purpose of this book, we will focus on ritual words and sounds—whether in the form of prayers, songs, or chants. This can also include the ancient god and goddess names—which can be signals to the corresponding archetype. These applications can also include childhood prayers, affirmations, and even chants.

Regardless of the form of the sacred sound, it is important to use the correct technique, a process called toning, that is essential to eliciting the most dynamic effect. This process includes the silent and the audible in conjunction with the in-breath and out-breath.

1. As you inhale, say the divine name, the chant, or the first line of the prayer silently, drawing out each syllable or word and giving it equal emphasis.

---

[3] For informatioin on healing with music and sound, refer to my earlier books, *Music Therapy for Non-Musicians* (Dragonhawk Publishing, 1997) and *Sacred Sounds* (Llewellyn Publications, 1992).

2. Hold the breath as long as is comfortable.

3. Exhale slowly, toning the divine name, chant, or first line of the chosen prayer slowly but audibly, drawing out each syllable or word and giving each equal emphasis.

4. As you do this, focus and visualize the associated energy being released and activated in your life.

5. Inhale, silent. Exhale, audible. In. Out. The spiritual to the physical.

When our prayers, our chants, and our affirmations are performed in this way for 10 to 15 minutes, the energy activated is astounding. The aura brightens and strengthens. We are cleansed. The energy associated with the divine names, using the proper toning method, intensifies the chant or prayer. The method described above was used in most traditions, and today it is known as "Directed Esoteric Toning."

The names and descriptive energies associated with gods, goddesses, and archangels that we can call upon for protection are listed in Chapter 10. Their names are links to corresponding archetypal forces; by toning them, we dynamically release their energies into our life.

Also use common mantras and prayers of childhood. There are many books providing a variety of chants and prayerful affirmations to energize and protect ourselves. When we use them with the directed esoteric toning technique, their effectiveness increases, they can also be used for quick energy fixes.

EXERCISE: 𝕿𝖍𝖊 𝕽𝖔𝖘𝖊𝖘 𝖔𝖋 𝕷𝖎𝖌𝖍𝖙

> **BENEFITS:**
> - balancing to all systems of the body and all chakras
> - healing and strengthening to the aura
> - relieves stress and worry

This exercise is wonderfully and gently healing and empowering.[4] It restores balance throughout the body and alleviates stress. The meditation is greatly enhanced by using rose incense or oil.

Music played softly in the background can also enhance the effects. If unsure what music to play, use none, but some of the types of music that are generally protective and strengthening, and suitable include:

- Gregorian chants
- Native American chants and songs
- drones (bagpipes, crystal bowls, etc.)
- chants and religious songs of our heritage

---

[4] This exercise is available on audio cassette and can be ordered through your local bookstore. For more information, see pages 356-357.

PREPARATION

Make yourself comfortable. Take the phone off the hook and ensure that you will not be disturbed. Light the rose incense or anoint yourself or the room with rose oil.

Perform a progressive relaxation. Start at the bottom of the feet and visualize sending warm soothing energy to each part of the body. Slowly work your way up to the top of the head. Take your time with this. The more relaxed you are, the greater the benefits.

THE MEDITATION

1. Now visualize a tiny spark of crystalline **red light at the base of the spine**.

    As you do, it shimmers and dances, forming itself into a small pastel red rosebud within you. As you breathe slowly and easily, that red rose bud begins to unfold petal by petal. As it opens within you, streams of crystalline red light and energy stream out. It fills the body, and it touches every cell within you to heal and balance, strengthen and bless.

    See and feel the RED ROSE OF NEW LIFE blossoming within you.

2. Now bring your attention **to the area of the navel. There a tiny spark of crystalline orange** light begins to shimmer and dance.

    As you focus upon it, it becomes a soft pastel orange rosebud within you. It begins to unfold petal by petal, sending streams of crystalline orange light and energy throughout the body.

EXERCISE:

It touches every cell within you to heal and balance, strengthen and bless.

See and feel the ORANGE ROSE OF NEW JOY blossoming within you.

3. Now there appears **a tiny yellow spark of light in the area of the solar plexus.**

   As you focus upon it, it becomes a pastel yellow rose bud. It begins to unfold within you petal by petal, sending streams of crystalline yellow light and energy throughout the body. That light touches every cell within you to heal and balance, strengthen and bless.

   See and feel the YELLOW ROSE OF TRUTH AND KNOWLEDGE blossoming within you.

4. Next there appears **a tiny emerald green spark of light in the area of the heart.**

   As you focus upon it, it shimmers and dances and transforms itself into a soft emerald rose bud. It too begins to unfold within you, petal by petal, sending streams of soft emerald light and energy throughout the body. That light touches every cell, to heal and balance, strengthen and bless.

   See and feel the EMERALD ROSE OF NEW HARMONY blossoming within you.

The Roses of Light

5. In the area of the throat **a tiny pale blue spark of light shimmers** and dances.

   As you focus upon it, it becomes a soft sky blue rosebud. It too begins to unfold within you, petal by petal, sending streams of soft blue light throughout the body. It touches every cell within you to heal and balance, strengthen and bless.

   See and feel the BLUE ROSE OF CREATIVE WILL blossoming within you.

6. Now there appears **in the area of the brow, a soft indigo spark of light**.

   As you focus upon it, it shimmers and dances, becoming a deep indigo rosebud. It too begins to unfold, sending streams of crystalline indigo light throughout the body, to heal and balance, strengthen and bless.

   See and feel the INDIGO ROSE OF HIGHER VISION blossoming within you.

7. Then **at the crown of the head there appears a violet spark of light**.

   It too shimmers and dances, becoming a violet rosebud within you. As you focus upon it, it begins to unfold, sending streams of crystalline violet light and energy throughout the body. It touches every cell within you, to heal and balance, strengthen and bless.

   See and feel the VIOLET ROSE OF TRANSFORMATION blossoming within you.

EXERCISE:

8.   You have now formed within you the **seven roses of light.**

As you focus upon them, together they stream forth their energies filling the body with rainbow light and energy. It fills the body and flows out to encircle you. Your entire aura is shimmering with rainbow light that heals and balances, strengthens and blesses.

See and feel yourself as the LIVING RAINBOW ROSE OF LIGHT!

The Roses of Light

ROSES OF LIGHT AUDIO CASSETTE
The music was composed specifically to balance all chakras and major systems of the body, and the visualization was created to enhance the effects of the music.

Chapter 8

Protection through Nature

*What is particularly intriguing, in fact, is that whereas
many peoples tend to locate this experience
of the sacred in certain unusual,
if not "supernatural" moments and circumstances...
the Oriental focus is upon mystery in the most obvious,
ordinary, mundane—the most natural—situations of life.*

Conrad Hyers

Nature is probably our greatest healing resource. From the plants we gain medicines and beauty. From the trees we get fruit and strength. The stones gift us with color, light, and electrical frequencies of health. The animals guide, teach, and protect us. We are blessed by Nature.

There was a time when we recognized ourselves as part of the natural world. Although nature is still today a sacred place of healing, protection, and wonder, most people have lost their intimate connection to it and to its inhabitants.

In our modern society, we have separated ourselves from the natural world. What we fail to remember is that we are part of Nature, and no matter how much we cloak ourselves in civilization, we are linked to it. Everything that happens within the natural world has repercussions upon us and everything that happens to us has repercussions upon the natural world. If we remember that we are tied to nature, we can draw more easily upon her energies for strength, healing, and protection at any time.

Every aspect of Nature can provide healing and protection. From the elements to the animals, from the plants and trees to stones and minerals, Nature is one of our most powerful guardians and healers!

Every tree has stories and wisdom. Every plant has healing and every animal has spirit. Every cycle brings opportunity for change and growth. The air is filled with familiar and exotic fragrances that tease and delight. The songs of birds awaken and soothe. The colors of plants, flowers, and trees resonate subtly with our body and mind. Even the appearance of an animal can cause our spirit to soar.

At one time or another in our lives, Nature has touched us in personal but special ways. Nature reminds us that there are things much greater than the affairs of humans. When we are unbalanced or if life is unsettled around us, whether through erratic psychic activities or through day-to-day life aggravations, we can do no better for ourselves than to seek out the embrace of Nature.

EXERCISE: 𝕿𝔥𝔢 𝖀𝔞𝔠𝔯𝔢𝔡 𝖂𝔞𝔩𝔨

BENEFITS:
- grounding and stabilizing
- puts life and situations into perspective
- calms fears
- heals and blesses

We cannot explore anything within the new age and metaphysical realm without coming across someone who recommends hugging a tree. Whether we choose to hug them or just sit under them, at some point we begin to realize that trees (and every aspect of Nature) are living creatures.

> It eats, rests, breathes and circulates its 'blood' much as we do. The heartbeat of a tree is a wonderful crackling, gurgling flow of life. The best time to hear the forest heartbeat is in early spring, when the trees send first surges of sap upward to their branches, preparing them for another season of growth.[1]

---

[1] Joseph Cornell. *Sharing Nature With Children.* (Nevada City, NV: Dawn Publications, 1979), p.22.

Exercise:

Yes, hugging a tree does have physiological and psychological benefits, but we do not have to hug it to experience its energies—its personality. Our aura will interact with the auras and energies of everything within Nature. I spoke earlier of the pines and willows, but every tree, plant, stone, and animal has its own qualities, its own energies. We cannot walk through Nature without realizing the life and energy within every aspect of her.

One of the most beneficial ways to eliminate stress and to strengthen our entire aura is to take a sacred nature walk. Choose a park or woods in your area. Even city parks are beneficial for this. Try to choose a place where there are trees and natural trails (no concrete walkways unless it is all that is available). Try to pick a place that also has a stream, river, or lake nearby. By choosing a place with trees, meadows, and natural water, we balance all of the elements within the body. Our own earth, water, air, and fire become balanced and strengthened.

Plan to have at least an hour for this exercise, and I highly recommend it be a gift to yourself at least once a week. The best times are early morning and dusk because more animals are active and more likely to be experienced. If it cannot be done at these times, any time will provide benefit.

Treat your walk as something sacred, a spiritual realigning of your body and its essence with Mother Nature. Do not anticipate what you should expect to encounter. The idea is not to try and encounter anything in particular, but to merge with Nature, to awaken and heal our senses and energies. Try

The Sacred Walk

to plan your walk so that it gives you time in different types of environment—open areas, trees, and water.

1. **Feel the earth beneath your feet.**

   As you step out along the trail you have chosen, feel the earth beneath your feet. If your area has only a concrete walkway or bike path, step off of it onto the earth itself periodically, so you have direct contact with the earth. If it is warm enough, at some point take your shoes and socks off so that your skin touches the earth directly.

   Notice whether the earth is soft or hard. By doing this in the beginning, we will notice changes in the terrain more naturally as they are encountered. Know that with each step you are grounded and stabilized, no matter what the terrain. Know that this groundedness and stabilizing will touch all aspects of your life when you leave.

2. **Pause periodically and breathe deeply.**

   Periodically along your walk, pause and breathe deeply, inhaling the fragrances and the air. Notice how sweet it is and how good it feels to breathe the air of Nature. Know that with each breath your aura becomes cleaner, freer of stress. It becomes more vibrant.

3. **Listen to the sounds around you.**

   Can you hear the song of birds? The humming and buzzing of insects? Listen to the sound of your feet on the earth. Every sound awakens your own inner symphony. It makes us more alert and perceptive.

EXERCISE:

4. Stop when something catches you attention.

As you walk along your sacred path, stop whenever something catches your attention. The flash of
sunlight on the water, the brightness of a flower,
the dance of a butterfly. Quietly note the colors
that stand out for you and know that you are
absorbing all of the colors of Nature into you with
each step you take.

5. Feel the sun and the air upon you.

Feel it energizing you, increasing your circulation
making you more vibrant. Touch things as you
walk. Let your hands brush the leaves of a tree.
Feel the roughness and strength of trees. Feel the
daintiness of a spring beauty, so tiny and yet
powerful enough to grow among such diverse life.

6. Know that you are healed.

Step to the water's edge. Hear the stream and feel
it. It may even whisper to you. Feel your own
blood moving in rhythm with it. Feel yourself
cleansed by being in its presence. Know that you
are healed.

The Sacred Walk

As your walk draws to a close, note how much more alive your senses are. The air is sweeter, the colors brighter, the sounds crisper, all because we have grounded and energized ourselves through Nature. Feel all of your elements balanced and healed.

Make a mental note of anything that stood out for you on your walk. Before the day is over, study some of its significance. The symbology of it will often provide wonderful insight into things occurring within our life. Offer a small prayer of thanks for the blessing. Know that the benefits will grow throughout the day and with each return visit.

EXERCISE:

ENERGY AND SYMBOLISM OF TREES

Tree	Energy
ASH	might, immortality, a universal source of life
ASPEN	calms anxieties, tree of resurrection, soul fearlessness, communication
APPLE	healing energies, promotes happiness, open to Faerie Realm and the unicorn
BEECH	awakens tolerance; aids contact to higher self, beneficial for all times of growth
BIRCH	staffs of birch used by shamans to open doorways to different dimensions, healing
CEDAR	protective, healing to emotional and astral imbalances
CHERRY	insights and openness, Tree of the Phoenix, threshold of new awakening
CYPRESS	healing, understanding of crises, awakens comfort of home
ELDER	protection and healing, mysteries of all burial rites
ELM	lends strength, aids overcoming exhaustion, awakens intuition, contact with Nature spirits

The Sacred Walk

ENERGY AND SYMBOLISM OF TREES (CONT.)

Tree	Energy
EUCALYPTUS	cleansing to aura during psychic growth, protective and healing
FIG	releases past life blockages, opens correct perspective, sacred tree of Buddha
HAWTHORNE	fertility, growth, creativity, sacred to the fairies
HAZEL	magickal tree of hidden wisdom, hazel twigs make great dowsing instruments
HOLLY	protection, awakens love and overcomes hate, birth of Christ within
HONEYSUCKLE	helps learning from the past, energy of change, sharpens intuition and psychic abilities
LEMON	cleansing to the aura, draws protective spirits, good for purification at full moon
LILAC	spiritualizes intellect, mental clarity, draws good spirits
MAPLE	balances yin and yang, draws prosperity and love, grounding to psychic energies
MAGNOLIA	energy top locate lost ideas, thoughts, or items; aligns the heart and mind
MISTLETOE	sacred to Druids, awakens female energy, protects children or the child within

EXERCISE: The Sacred Walk

ENERGY AND SYMBOLISM OF TREES (CONT.)

Tree	Energy
OAK	sacred to Druids, awakens male energy, strength, endurance, helpfulness
OLIVE	tree of peace and harmony, restores peace of mind, regeneration, enables the touching of inner guidance
ORANGE	balancing to astral energy, brings clarity to emotions
PALM	tree of peace, protection of an area or group, leaves prevent evil from entering an area
PEACH	calms emotions, awakens artistic energies, helps realize ultimate spiritual immortality
PINE	calms emotions, awakens occult salvation, understanding, sacred tree of Mithra and Dionysus
SYCAMORE	brings life and gifts, nourishment and beauty, sacred tree of Hathor and Egyptians
WALNUT	hidden wisdom, power for transition, catalytic energy, frees the spirit, helps us to follow our path
WILLOW	healing, removes aches and pains, flexibility, clarifies links between our thoughts and external events

Holly

EXERCISE: 𝔄doptïng tlje 𝔄daptïbe 𝔅eljabïor of our 𝔄nïmal 𝔊uardïans

> **BENEFITS:**
> - attunement to Nature
> - increased skill at handling opposition
>
> NOTE: specific benefits will vary according to the individual animal

Every animal in Nature has adaptative behaviors it uses to protect itself and to defend its territory. Some animals use physical adaptations, and other animals use behavioral adaptations.

Physical adaptations are such things as the bright colors found on some insects as a warning to predators that if they try and eat them it will leave a bad taste in their mouth. Some caterpillars have white spots or blotches on their backs that resemble the splatter of bird droppings. Since their most common predator is a bird, this is a physical adaptation that will help prevent birds from eating them. A bird will never eat something that has been defecated on.

Some animals in Nature have behavioral adaptations. Rabbits, for example, have a wonderful ability to remain still if they feel danger is close by. Most predators recognize prey by movement, so a rabbit's ability to freeze is an adaptive behavior for avoiding becoming someone's meal.

In an earlier book of mine, *Animal-Speak*, I explored the natural behaviors and aspects of a multitude of animals and what they reflect mystically and spiritually. We cannot possibly hope to examine them in this work, but we do need to remember that every animal, from a tiny mouse to an eagle, has ways of defending itself and protecting its home.

We must keep in mind that no animal in Nature is any more powerful or spiritual than any other animal. They all have their own unique characteristics. So if you assume that a large predator is what you should work with in psychic protection, you will probably find yourself in for an interesting educational lesson.

Most people would think that a hawk would have no trouble with a rabbit, and yet jack rabbits have been known to drag hawks, talons sunk into their backs, into their holes and kick the hawks to death.

A great horned owl is one of the most powerful and aggressive birds of prey. A single crow may not be able to handle it, but a flock of crows will mob an owl to drive it away. If we are working with crows to defend and protect ourselves, we will be ineffective by ourselves. The crow teaches us to join with others.

If we learn how our spirit animal or totem defends itself, we can then apply it to our own life. That animal has shown up to be a part of our life, to tell us, "These behaviors I have are what will work for you right now. Use them!" When we do, we find everything coming together and falling into place. We find it easier to accomplish our goals with less trouble.

EXERCISE:

We are part of Nature, and as most traditions upon this planet taught, the animals are our brothers and sisters. We can, by aligning with nature and by determining our spirit totems, apply their defenses to our own life with great success.

PREPARATION

Begin by choosing an appropriate animal to help with your protection.[2] There are a lot of ways of determining what our spirit animals are or what animal is most important to us for the situation at hand. Nature talks to us all the time. We have just forgotten how to listen. Begin by asking yourself some basic questions:

- What animals have you most been drawn to your entire life or most recently?
- Are there certain animals you keep seeing, even if only in your dreams?
- When you are in Nature, what animal stood out?
- Was there a particular bird that was squawking?
- Did you see anything unusual when you were outside in Nature?

Take a look at the animals in your own back yard. Those animals already living within your environment have learned

---

[2] This is not a book for discovering our spirit totems. There are books in the bibliography that can help. An audio cassette of mine, *Discover Your Spirit Animal*, can also be beneficial.

Adopting the Adaptive Behavior of our Animal Guardians

to do so successfully. Studying how they accomplish this will be beneficial to you, showing you how to live more effectively within this same environment.

If you do not know your spirit animal, meditate on the problem and then take a walk in nature for about an hour. It can be a park or some other natural environment where there is wildlife. Usually by the end of that walk, some animal has gotten our attention several times. If unsure, wait 24 hours. Within 24 hours that animal will have shown itself 3 to 4 times around you. You may see it outside, or on a TV program, but there will be 3 to 4 encounters.

Go to the library and learn as much about that animal as possible. Jot down its predators as well as those creatures it preys upon. Most animals in the wild are both predators and prey.

Learn About Adapting Behaviors

Study how the animal defends its home. This is the most important clue as to how our animal guardians use adaptive behavior. Does it do it alone? Does it have help? Does it hide? Does it camouflage itself? How does it defend and protect itself? This animal has gotten your attention to teach you how to apply these same tactics to your life.

If you have someone or something troubling you, this animal's natural tactics will help. If it is an opossum, you might have to develop some play-acting skills around certain individuals so they do not know your business or what is truly going on. Some animals put on a intense show of strength and power as a warning to intruders. If we have spirits that are

EXERCISE:

aggravating us, we may have to put on a stronger display and assert greater control. We must find a way of applying the animal's natural defense tactics to our individual situation.

Examine Where You Are Having Difficulty

Make a list of people that may be troubling you, or of whom you may have suspicions. Are there certain happenings or phenomena that are unsettling. Are you feeling unbalanced? Write down the ideas.

As you are doing this, focus on the animal and its behavior. Ask yourself how this animal would handle such a situation, realizing that the animal is the solution.

- Would it hide until the trouble goes away and passes?

- Would it camouflage itself?

- Would it confront with a display of ferocity?

- Would it join with others of its kind to handle the situation?

Adopting the Adaptive Behavior of our Animal Guardians

TO PERFORM THIS EXERCISE:

1. Join with the animal by finding a time when you will not be disturbed—preferably outdoors, if possible.

2. Visualize the animal appearing before you, its eyes looking into your eyes.

3. Study this animal's eyes and realize that this creature has your eyes—that it is your eyes looking out of it at you.

4. Allow the animal to melt into you. With each breath that you take, its essence grows stronger inside of you. You feel as it feels. Your senses are alive.

5. Allow the animal to grow stronger within you, seeing yourself handling all of the problems in the same way this animal would.

6. Allow your imagination to run with it.

Although it may seem as if its a fanciful past time, the effects will be very real over the next three days. Opportunities to correct situations that are out of balance will arise. The tactics this animal would use are what will work for you.

EXERCISE:

BENEFITS:

- assertiveness with problems, control over energies
- resolution of problems, strong protection
- patience and sharpened senses in cases of psychic attack

Predators and prey are found everywhere in nature. A predator is defined as one who has the ability to take live prey. There has always been a contest between predator and prey in the natural world, and life is always the prize. The grasshopper eats the grass and the frog eats the grasshopper. The snake eats the frog and the hawk eats the snake.

Predation takes time, patience, and skill. It sharpens the senses. The strongest, most alert, and most knowledgeable will survive. Animals grow stronger and wiser trying to avoid being caught.

This simple visualization is a powerful tool for protection. It may seem uncomplicated, but in its simplicity, it has even greater effectiveness. For this exercise you will need to choose a predator animal. This may be an animal you know is already one of your totems. It may be an animal you have

Aligning with our Predator Guardians

always had an affinity for. It may be an animal you have dreamt of. It may be an animal you choose out of the blue.

Only spend 5 to 10 minutes a day on this exercise, but put a lot of passion into it.

PREPARATION

Choose your predator and study it. Go to the library and research the following questions to learn more about the animal's predator's instincts:

- How does it attack and defend?

- What kind of natural weapons and skills does it have?

- When hunting, what skills does it rely upon?

- What is its most common prey?

- What animal does it eat?

- What tactics will its prey most likely use to avoid being caught?

The last question is most important. By understanding how the prey is more likely to respond, by understanding how it naturally behaves, we can use that to our advantage.

When performing the following exercise, use the predator's natural hunt cycle and tactics in this meditation. If it hunts primarily at night and by stalking, perform the exercise at night. If it hunts during the day, perform it during

EXERCISE:

the day. Within a week, you will begin to notice a difference. Problems and stresses will begin to ease up. Psychic imbalances will settle. Make sure that you see yourself stronger, healthier, and more empowered as a result of this exercise.

TO PERFORM THIS EXERCISE

1. **Prepare for the meditation.**

   Make sure that you will be undisturbed. The phone should be off the hook. You might want to use a candle or fragrance to enhance the meditation. Perform a progressive relaxation. The more relaxed you are the more effective it will be.

2. **Visualize a bad habit, an uncomfortable situation or something negative around you as the natural prey.**

3. **Visualize yourself as the predator.**

   See yourself sitting out in nature and this predator stepping out in front of you. It fixes you with its eyes, and you realize that it has your eyes. Your eyes are looking out of it at you! As you realize this, it melts into you, and with each breath you see and feel yourself as this predator. It does not just live within you and you in it. You are the predator.

Aligning with our Predator Guardians

4. Hunt, capture, and eat your prey.

Visualize the prey before you, and with the hunting tactics of the predator you are, you attack. See and feel yourself capturing, killing, and eating the bad habit, negative attitude, the unbalanced psychic energy, eliminating it from your life.

5. Feel yourself becoming stronger as a result.

Predator

Chapter 9

Protection through Sacred Shields

When you are inspired by some great purpose,
some extraordinary project, all your thoughts
break their bounds: your mind transcends limitations, your
consciousness expands in every direction and
you will find yourself in a new, great and wonderful world.
Dormant forces, faculties and talents become alive,
and you discover yourself to be a greater person by far
than you ever dreamed yourself to be.

Patanjali

Shields have an ancient history. Their creation, decoration, and application are varied, but in most societies the shield was as much practical as it was symbolic and sacred. Most people are familiar with the European shields, the Coat of Arms, and the medicine shields of the Native Americans. Both served multiple functions as did the decorated shields in many societies throughout the world. Their primary function was protection.

In Europe, heraldry became more formalized, but its origins and significance is just as symbolic as in those societies in which the methods were less formal. In most societies, heraldry (the creation and decorating of shields) was associated with armorial bearing and originally it served a practical purpose. Painting the shields helped to identify opponents in battle. Since the shields had a simple flat surface, this created a practical place for painting.

TYPICAL EUROPEAN HERALDIC SHIELD

Many believe that the European heralds were originally minstrels familiar with the various coats of arms and those who bore them. They came to serve an exaggerated function during tournaments and jousts. During these medieval times, heraldry developed its own descriptive language and rules. In other parts of the world, it would remain less formalized but just as significant, as epitomized by the medicine shield of the Native Americans:

> A shield reflected the symbology of a warrior's medicine. "Medicine" to the plains tribes carried a broader scope in its meaning than simple healing of physical affliction or injury. Medicine reached into all facets of a person's life. Protection in combat, success in the hunt, success in lovemaking and mate selection, protection from evil doing, and success in visions and dreams were major petitions and were reflected in the symbols found on the Sioux shields.[1]

---

[1] Ed McGaa, Eagle Man, *Mother Earth Spirituality* (San Francisco, CA: Harper, 1990), p. 158.

As in heraldry, the medicine shields could be simple or intricate. They could represent family, tribe, or the individual. Unlike the shields of Europe, the medicine shields were usually circular, representing the never-ending cycle of life, death, and rebirth—no beginning and no end. This circular shield reflects the Medicine Wheel, the Sacred Loop—the symbol of all of life's cycles.

Animals, real and mythical, that were significant to the individual would often appear. These are totems and the shield bearer established a relationship with them by becoming familiar with the animal's unique characteristics. The animal totem could also be a special spirit helper to the person, providing protection, as discussed in Chapter 8. The picture of a protective animal on the shield becomes a way of invoking its energy.

Recurring dreams and visions could be represented on the shield. Colors which reflect specific qualities were used in their creation. A person's

Native American Medicine Shield Design

special gifts or uniqueness could appear on a shield in a symbolic manner. Shields are ceremonial, religious, spiritual, and armorial. There are shields for countries, counties, towns, cities, and families. We can have shields for different aspects of our life, or a shield that encompasses all.

There is no limit to the number or types of shields we can have. We can create a shield for protection or a shield for healing. We can create a spirit shield for our work with other realms and dimensions. We can create a personal shield reflecting all aspects of ourselves, spiritual and physical. For our purposes, we will focus primarily on the shield of protection, although its construction and the manner in which it works applies to all shields.

Whatever kind of shield we make or however we construct it, there are three principles to keep in mind throughout the creation process:

1. The creating and making of the shield activates your stronger creative life forces. This strengthens your aura and increases your vitality, starting the process of shielding yourself from outside forces.

2. The shield speaks of you and who you are.

3. All things made deliberately are accurate mirrors reflecting those who make them and the forces represented upon them.

Although some societies had formalized rules for making shields, it is not necessary to follow rigid formulas. Shields can be made from any material and can be constructed from metal or cloth, drawn on paper, or painted on a wall. They can be whatever shape we believe is most significant for its purpose.

Whether we actually construct a shield or simply sketch or paint one, the process is powerful. On one level they become talismans, yantras, or mandalas. Mandalas and yantras are geometric designs created to express and invoke specific archetypal energies in the physical or the spiritual realms, awakening a sense of our relationship to ourselves and to the forces of the universe represented on them. They provide bridges to archetypal forces, linking the physical and spiritual dimensions.

Mandalas hold the essence of a thought or a concept, and are designed to draw our consciousness more fully into that concept, stimulating our inner creative forces in a manner peculiar to its design. Shields, like mandalas, can be constructed to arouse any inner force we desire, possibly becoming a tool for integration and transformation or a tool of action and interaction with ourselves and our life.

When we create a sacred shield of protection, several things will automatically occur. We will find ourselves and our environment strengthened and protected since the shield becomes a mirror, reflecting its protective qualities into our life more dynamically. As the elements for the shield are brought together, balance and harmony begin to manifest during the construction process. While it is being made, aggravations begin to disappear and that which had not been working begins to work once more as flow and balance begin to be restored.

Simple ideas for create your own sacred shield of protection include:

- Do not limit the creation of your shield to the ideas presented here.

- Study heraldry, which will provide some wonderful inspiration.

- Follow your own heart in the design, using your creative energies and you will find each shield you create becomes more powerful and significant.

Common Heraldic and Medicine Shield Symbols

The following pages contain basic symbology and correspondences for sacred shield making. Two traditions are represented, the European Heraldic Tradition and the Native American Medicine Shield Tradition, which can be beneficial for creating our own sacred shield of protection.

Different native peoples had their own correspondences in colors and animals. These were used in making the medicine shields. If you have ancestors linked to a particular tribe, you may find it especially beneficial to study their correspondences. If you are drawn to a particular tradition, you should study it as well. The more significance you can realize, the greater the power your shield will have for you.

Remember that the making of the shield itself is a sacred process, and the more thought and focus we put into it, the greater its power. Everything we put on our shield will have significance. It is good to know why we select certain colors.

Keep in mind also that the shield may change in the construction process.

TRADITIONAL HERALDIC
VOCABULARY

BLAZON	the language used to describe shields of arms, crests & badges
DEXTER	the left side of the shield (as it is faced)
SINISTER	the right side of the shield (as it is faced)
FIELD	the surface of the shield
PER PALE	shield field that is divided vertically
PER FESS	shield field that is divided horizontally
PER BEND	shield field that is divided diagonally
PER CROSS	shield field divided into quarters
PER SALTIRE	shield field with multiple lines (diagonal)
ORDINARIES	principle shapes
CHARGES	significant animals, mythical beasts or inanimate objects. The animals were usually in one of four positions:

1. **rampant**: standing on one hind leg
2. **passant**: walking past
3. **displayed**: outstretched wings
4. **sejant**: seated erect

Although we may initially decide on a predominant color, once we get started, we may find that it doesn't quite suit us. HONOR THAT FEELING!

Also remember that the creation of the shield is never truly completed. Over several months or even years, we may add new images, variations, and colors. This simply reflects our growth and new depths we are achieving. I have several shield designs I created years ago that I am still adding to periodically. My totem animal shield has a multitude of creatures on it, added to over the years. These animals include my own power totems, but also other wild life which has appeared in my life at significant times and for special purposes.

Additions to spiritual and protection shields are natural. They reflect changes in spiritual growth and perception. New symbols and variations will be added as our own spiritual depths expand. Change is part of life and reflects an increasing variety of forces which are significant to us, forces we have learned or are learning to draw upon and use within our day-to-day life.

TRADITIONAL HERALDIC CHARGES

ANCHOR	=	faith
APPLE	=	good luck
ARM	=	power
ARROW	=	authority
AXE	=	strength
BEAR	=	defender
BEE	=	industrious
BOAT	=	venture
BULL	=	protecto
BOAR	=	perseverance
CRANE	=	vigilance
CROSS	=	dedication
CROWN	=	royalty
DOG	=	fidelity
DOVE	=	faith
EAGLE	=	superiority
HEART	=	gentleness
HORSE	=	speed
KEY	=	knowledge
KNIFE	=	sacrifice
LION	=	strength
MACE	=	authority
PELICAN	=	sacrifice and faith
SERPENT	=	defiance
STAG	=	purity
TOWER	=	defense
UNICORN	=	virtue
DRAGON	=	knowledge & power

EXERCISE: 𝕸aking 𝕐our 𝕾acred 𝕻ower 𝕾hield

BENEFITS:

- protection
- healing
- activation of creative life force
- strength and balance

Initially, we will want to draw or sketch our shield prior to actually constructing it. Even the simple act of drawing a design will actualize the energies associated with it. Anytime we do something physical like this, we are drawing those forces out of that vague ethereal realm and setting them in motion more dynamically within our physical life.

Concentration in the creating of the shield is important. Prior to actually starting, we may wish to meditate upon the creation of a shield, and once we start the construction, we must make sure we will be undisturbed while working. Take as many precautions as necessary to avoid interruptions. The creation of the shield is an active meditation in itself. We are activating the right brain, programming it to respond to the images, symbols, and significance of the shield and all of its reflective energies.

1. **Begin by gathering together your materials.**

    You will need drawing utensils, paper, scissors, etc. If you cannot draw (or feel that you can't), obtain pictures of the protective animals that you can trace or cut out—if you are choosing to use animals. Do the same thing with any other protective symbols—be they animals, colors, geometric shapes, or symbols of the various gods and goddesses to which you have an affinity.

    Some of the symbols and images of Divine beings from other traditions are found in the Chapter 10. Since this shield is for protection and balance, I have provided only those beings and their symbols associated with protection and balance. The technique for making protective angelic amulets in Chapter 10 can also be easily adapted to making angelic shields.

NATIVE AMERICAN & SHAMANIC SHIELD SYMBOLS
(DIRECTIONS)

Seneca Tradition

EAST	air; mind; creativity; yellow
SOUTH	fire; inspiration; purification; red
WEST	water; emotion; intuition; blue
NORTH	earth; body; prosperity; green

Sioux Tradition

EAST	wind; wolf; red hawk; red
SOUTH	fire; buffalo; bear; yellow
WEST	water; thunderbird; black horse; black
NORTH	earth; eagle; snowy owl; white

Chippewa Tradition

EAST	spring; eagle; red and gold
SOUTH	summer; coyote; green and yellow
WEST	autumn; grizzly bear; deep blues and black
NORTH	winter; white buffalo; white

If you intend to only draw the shield rather than actually make one, you will want to draw it the size of poster board. This will make it easier to hang and focus upon in meditation.

EXERCISE:

2. **Determine the colors.**

    Choose colors that are your favorite or that you find calming and protective to yourself. Choose the various angelic beings, gods, and goddesses whose protective energies you wish to invoke through the shield. I have provided corresponding colors.

    You may even want to use opposite colors as they balance each other: red and green, black and white, orange and blue, purple and gold. When you choose the colors, learn something about their hidden significance. Most colors are symbolic, and studying them may reveal much about yourself and the energies you will be invoking through this shield.

TRADITIONAL HERALDIC COLORS		
GULES	=	red (fire and fortitude)
OR	=	gold (purity and valor)
AZURE	=	blue (loyalty and truth)
ARGENT	=	white (peace and nobility)
VERT	=	green (strength and freshness)
PURPURE	=	purple (justice, majesty, royalty)
SABLE	=	black (royalty and repentence)
ERMINE	=	black tails on white (valor and leadeship)
VAIR	=	pattern of blue and white (truth and purity)

3. **Decide on a basic shape for your shield.**

    It may be a typical heraldic shape or it can be any other shape. Again, the more significance we attach to the shape, the greater the effect. Geometric shapes affect electromagnetic patterns. They stimulate and elicit definable effects. If unsure, I suggest using a circular or square field for your shield since both can be effective for every type of shield that you might wish to create.

Making Your Sacred Power Shield

4. Create the shield.

Take your drawing paper or your poster board and draw the basic shield form (circle, square or whatever you have chosen) in the center. Leave enough space around the edges that you will be able to add images and other symbols. Some people like to place the animal totems inside the circle, while others like to put them outside. For some, the inner placement symbolizes the animals' energies alive and active within them. For others, the outer placement reflects their guardianship and protection of the life environment.

One is no better than the other. Whichever you choose, know why you do so. It adds power to the creation process and to its ultimate effectiveness.

Place in this shield the colors and other symbols that are significant to your life and to the purpose of

SHAPES AND THEIR SIGNIFICANCE	
circle	= wholeness, complete, circle of life, calmness
square	= balance, solidness, the four elements, stability
triangle	= power, amplification, energizing, strengthening
diamond	= creativity, activation, stimulating
crescent	= feminine, creative intuition, emotional calm
cross	= balance of elements, harmonizing polarities or opposites
six-rayed star	= healing, strengthening and protecting

this shield. Since this one is for protection and balance, ask yourself, "What other symbols and images do I associate with balance, health and protection?"

Arranging the symbols upon the shield is a creative process. Place them in the manner that is best for you. Just make sure that you know the purpose and significance of each. Use the colors in

EXERCISE:

the manner best for you as well. Place them in the different sections that you feel are appropriate.

Place something personal to you upon the shield. It should be in a central position. This is something that represents you. In this way the energies activated by the shield will flow into your life and center around you appropriately.

5. **Avoid being critical of your protection shield.**

The idea is not to demonstrate artistic abilities or lack of them. You are using the shield to tap into archetypal energies and to draw them out and manifest them more dynamically.

Early shamans and primitive peoples are not considered artistically gifted, but their shields and drawings were imbued with a significance and power that was very primal. As you infuse the making of the shield and all of its elements with significance, it will attain its own beauty and primal power.

6. **Feel free to add to your shield from time to time.**

If you reach a point where you are not sure what to add, just stop. You have probably created one that is suitable for you at the moment. Trust that it will evolve and change as you do.

The shield will take on a life of its own as you construct or draw it. This is good! It's a positive sign the shield is already working.

You will also find in the process that you lose track of time. This is also a positive sign that you have touched and activated those archetypal energies

Making Your Sacred Power Shield

associated with the symbols of the shield. You have been drawn into their energy.

7. Meditate with the shield.

When you finish the drawing or construction the shield, set it across the floor from you and just gaze softly upon it and all of its elements for 10 to 15 minutes. Feel its energies. Review in your mind its many significances. Visualize it working for you. See events changing, harmonizing, and balancing.

Know that by its construction you have released the energy of balance into your physical life and that the shield will work.

Over the next several days or even a week, you may feel that some changes in your shield are necessary. Follow through on them.

When you are satisfied, you may wish to hang the drawing where you can see it everyday, or you may wish to construct an actual shield. This can be done with cloth, wood, metal, or any of a variety of things, depending upon how much time and effort you wish to put into it.

8. Hang your drawing or your shield in a prominent place.

The shield should always be displayed. This keeps the door open to the archetypal forces represented in it. By having it visibly displayed, every glance upon it releases more of its energy into our life. It reminds us that we are guarded, guided, and blessed by the forces represented by it. It reminds us of the sacredness of our spirit.

Chapter 10

Protection through Awakening to the Divine

Gods do not think as men think. The thoughts of men are images; the thoughts of Gods are living beings!

Rudolph Steiner

By praying and wearing talismanic images (medals, stones, feathers, and so on), we can connect to other mysterious dimensions of the universe, forming a bridge to ask those archetypal forces for their protection.

Prayer is said to be a heightened state of awareness and communication. Prayer, through its language and symbolism, links us to archetypal forces and the divine. When we pray through word, movement or thought, we are working to unite ourselves to the divine in some manner for some purpose.

Prayer has been a part of all religious teachings, and new research tends to indicate a link between prayer and health.

Prayers can be simple or complicated, but their effectiveness depends upon the import and the power we attach to them. Our concepts of prayer have become distorted in modern times. Often they are little more than rote recitations or simple wish making. True prayer is the process of concentrated visualization, combined with mental and emotional energizing, leading to a union of body, mind, and spirit.

Prayer links us to the divine forces of the universe through a dialogue that institutes change. It is a dialogue with that part of us that resonates with the divine and has the ability to create or change any condition, according to our level of energy and consciousness.

For prayers to be effective on any level, there are three basic requirements. First, there must be proper visualization of what we are praying. We must see the situation as if our prayer is already answered. Secondly, there must also be an emotional energy attached to the prayer process. This is not the emotion of desiring, but rather of anticipating. Anticipate the answer to your prayer as if you have placed a catalog order and are simply waiting for UPS to drop it off to you.

The third, and most important part, is the grounding of the prayer into the physical. Because we are physical beings, we must apply physical energy to the praying process for it to work effectively. Sometimes this physical vocalization can be enough, but most of the time it is not. Without the physical aspect—the grounding of the prayer—the answer to our prayers may be delayed, hindered, and blocked.

The following two exercises are methods of physically grounding our prayers in very creative and dynamic ways. The first is an ancient technique associated with sacred dance ritual. The second falls in line with the idea of talismans and charms. We will show how to make an angelic amulet and explain why and how it will work, especially for protection.

EXERCISE: 𝕬wakening 𝕬ncient 𝕯ivine 𝕱orces

> ### BENEFITS:
> - spiritual guidance and protection
> - powerful alignment with divine forces

Every tradition and religion had its own rituals, music, and dance, its own means of awakening its members to the divine forces of that society's gods and goddesses. In all traditions, there were beings symbolic and representative of divine forces of protection and healing. There were also postures and dance movements created to honor these beings and invoke their energy.

A powerful means of employing movement to align with a particular divine force has come to be known as *Assumption of the God-Form*. In this process, we assume the identity of a specific deity.

The gods and goddesses of all religions have been depicted in art and literature. Centered around these images are powerful thoughtforms that have been created by all of the individuals who have worshipped and prayed to them. By

Exercise:

aligning ourselves with the deity through specific symbols, colors, costumes, posture, and other tools, we invoke the energy of that thoughtform into our lives more dynamically. We become the god or goddess for the purpose of the prayer. Through this identification process, we invoke the energy represented by the god-form. We use external appearances connected to the divine force to stimulate the subconscious into aligning us with those archetypal energies.

Assumption of the God-Form is a powerful tool, and it is important to understand the symbolism involved. If we are working with a particular tradition, it is beneficial to read and study the gods and goddesses to learn as much as possible about that tradition. The following pages contain the symbolism of major traditions and those being within them associated with protection and healing.

Preparation

In the beginning, study and learn as much about the tradition as possible. Keep in mind that most of the ancient gods and goddesses had positive and negative aspects, and unless we are aware of this, we may not be prepared for what we invoke. It is always best to start simply. The tables on the following pages provide information about some of the protectors from various cultural traditions.

You will also need to create your divine costume. This does not have to be difficult. Simply wearing the colors associated with the particular divinity will help create a shift in your own subconscious. Most people have things around the house that can be used. In the picture of me assuming the

𝔄wakening 𝔄ncient 𝔇ibine 𝔉orces

god-form of Apollo, I used things around the home. It only took about an hour to find the simple materials and set the tone.

1. **Set the tone.**

   Make sure you will be undisturbed by taking the phone off the hook. Light candles of colors associated with the particular being. Light incense or use an oil that is protective or even associated with the tradition you have chosen. Perform a progressive relaxation.

2. **Begin your prayer meditation.**

   Bring to mind the qualities and characteristics of the being you have selected. You may want to review particular tales and myths of this being's intercedence in the lives of others.

3. **Feel the energy of this being within you.**

   With each breath, see and feel yourself taking on the energy of this being AND BECOMING stronger, wiser. Feel yourself balanced and strengthened. See yourself shining. Some find it effective to see this being shining within their aura. Go with what makes you feel comfortable.

4. **Release the archetypal force into your life.**

   Now bring your attention to the problem at hand. See and feel the archetypal force of this being released into your life to calm storms, to protect and heal, to smooth out difficulties. Know that with the seeing of it, it will be done.

EXERCISE:

5. Bring the exercise to a close.

Visualize yourself linked to the divine. Feel yourself grounded and balanced. With each breath, see yourself in more control over your life. See this being and his or her energy encompassing you, your home, and all environments you walk. See and feel the energy of this being born within you— an energy that will empower your life!

6. Thank the divine force.

Offer a prayer out loud to the divinity for the protection and assistance in the days ahead. Thank the divine forces for making its presence known and felt clearly and increasingly from that day forth.

Awakening Ancient Divine Forces

Assuming the God-Form Apollo

EXERCISE:

CELTIC PROTECTORS FROM

Name	Known As	Symbols
DAGDA	patriarch father of the Celtic gods and goddesses	magic harp, cauldron that could never be emptied of its contents
CARRIDWEN	powerful in magic and prophecy	cauldron of wisdom
MORGAN LE FAY	the fairy queen	the hand extending the sword from the waters of life
BRIGID	strong goddess of guardianship	well of healing waters
RHIANNON	goddess of the horse	a pale gray horse, three sacred birds, bag of abundance
GWYDION	heroic god	all images of science and law
GWYN	night hunter	night, shadows, darkened doorways

Awakening Ancient Divine Forces

ANCIENT TRADITIONS

Associated With	Colors
protects against and destroys enemies, nourishes and reawakens inner strength	greens
source of our difficulties, teaches how to shapeshift	greens
protector of women and nature, her energy awakens purity, associated with healing magic	greens
assists those seeking their flame of life, awakens compassion and healing	greens
awakens assertiveness and justice, brings kindness, combats arrogance and cowardice	greens
awakens justice, awakens magical ability to settle legalities and injustices	greens
guardian of dark doorways of the mind, eases mental stress, reveals deceptions and shadows operating, reveals sources of difficulties through dreams	greens

EXERCISE:

EGYPTIAN PROTECTORS FROM

Name	Known As	Symbols
ISIS	goddess of moon and magic	throne, buckle, veil
THOTH	master of medicine, learning, and magic	caduceus
ANUBIS	protects travelers, finds lost things	jackal, sarcophagus

Awakening Ancient Divine Forces

ANCIENT TRADITIONS

Associated With	Colors
mother protector, especially for the young; can reveal names of those who threaten; full access to all magical knowledge	sky blue
most ancient teachings ascribed to him, can reveal fate and ward off misfortune	violet and amythyst
guards against lower astral energies, helps navigate dreams so essential information received, can reveal source of problems through dreams	black and silver

EXERCISE:

GREEK PROTECTORS FROM

Name	Known As	Symbols
ATHENA	warrior goddess of wisdom	helmet, shield, spear, owl
APOLLO	god of prophecy	bow and arrow, sun, lyre
ARTEMIS	huntress	bear, dog
ARES	warrior	all weapons

Awakening Ancient Divine Forces

ANCIENT TRADITIONS

Associated With	Colors
protects brave and awakens bravery, stimulates greater assertiveness in times of turmoil and difficulty	red and gold
awakens greater rebelliousness, great power over darkness, restores harmony and health, balances recklessness and wisdom	yellow and gold
psychic protection through animals and nature, protects children and animals sacred to her, safety and welfare of women, powerful against psychic attack	amethyst
protective power of nature and fertility, protects new ideas and projects, awakens discipline, helps slay the dragons within our lives	scarlet and red

Exercise:

Teutonic Protectors from

Name	Known As	Symbols
Odin	powerful and all-seeing	ravens, wolves, 8-legged steed, spear
Thor	god of thunder and lightning	hammer, iron mitt, belt of power
Tyr	bravest of gods	sacrificed hand
Heimdall	watchman	trumpet, horn, rainbow

Awakening Ancient Divine Forces

ANCIENT TRADITIONS

Associated With	Colors
reveals knowledge to help in times of difficulty, combats a lack of integrity, restores honor	deep blues, indigos
warrior god who comes to aid of all who call upon him, awakens inner strength, restores stability and bravery, champion of the common person	bright red
sacrifice for a higher cause, awakens greatest courage and strength in all situations aids in conquering all monsters	dark red of great strength
guards the rainbow bridge and thus guards our dreams, awakens far-sightedness to reveal source of problems and potential difficulties	colors of rainbow

EXERCISE: 𝕿𝖍𝖊 𝕬𝖓𝖌𝖊𝖑𝖎𝖈 𝕿𝖆𝖑𝖎𝖘𝖒𝖆𝖓

> ### BENEFITS:
> - angelic protection and emotional security
> - illuminating and strengthening to the aura

Talismans, such as a St. Christopher medal or a rosary, are symbols of specific energies we wish to attract. A person who is wearing a cross or a crystal about the neck is using a talismanic image as a physical reminder and a profession of his or her beliefs. Talismans serve as reminders and stimulators of creative forces.

Many of the oldest charms are derived from stones, feathers and herbs—things of nature. We know today that crystals have a form of electrical energy. Different crystals have different frequencies, and thus can be used for different things. Although there are many books available on how to use stones and crystal for protection and other purposes, we will not be examining them here.

Talismanic images serve several purposes. They awaken a sense of our relationship to the mysterious dimensions of the universe and help us to recognize and connect with those forces. They help us build a bridge to the archetypal forces.

The most effective talismans and amulets are those which are personally made. The process is neither complicated nor esoteric, but it is important to know why you are making them. The more significance you associate with the images and symbols, the more they will work for you. You must know what everything on the amulet represents and what forces each item is linked to.

All images, colors, symbols, and geometric shapes alter the electromagnetic field in which they exist, interacting with our own electromagnetic fields. For example, a pyramid shape amplifies other electromagnetic fields around it, which is why pyramid shapes are stimulating to the physical and spiritual energies of the individual. Thus talismans made in or using the pyramid shape will amplify the electromagnetic energy patterns represented by the talisman or amulet.

For this exercise we will show how to create a simple angelic amulet that we can wear for angelic protection. You will need the information on the symbolism of the four major archangels on the next page.

Talismans and amulets can be made of various materials: parchment, wood, paper, or cloth. Clean cotton is easy to work with. One side of our angelic amulet will have symbolism associated with a particular archangel, and the other side will be personalized, perhaps with your name or some symbol that represents you. Be as creative as possible.

EXERCISE:

1. **Take your cloth—either white cotton or the color associated with the archangel you have chosen.**

   Draw on it a double circle, each about two inches in diameter about a half an inch apart.

2. **On one of the two circles in the center draw the sigil, or name signature of the archangel.**

   This is a symbol representing the name of the angelic being, derived from old Qabalistic teachings and magical working with the Hebrew alphabet. You may wish to draw the sigil in the color associated with the archangel or even sew it on using appropriate colored thread.

3. **Arrange other symbols of protection that you find comforting around the symbol.**

   In the sample, I used the phases of the moon, to represent angelic protection in all phases and at all times.

4. **On the other circle draw or sew symbols personal to you.**

5. **Cut the talisman out of the cloth.**

   Do not cut the circles out separately. Leave them connected by a half-inch square section of cloth. Fold the talisman at the half inch square section and align the two circles so that the markings and symbols are facing out.

The Angelic Talisman

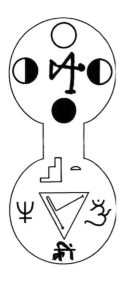

On one side of the material will be symbols and designs to stimulate whatever activity you are desiring.

On the other side of the talisman will be the personalized symbols and sigils, your name sigils, and any other sumbols you wish to employ

ANGELIC TALISMAN BEFORE FOLD

EXERCISE:

6. **Before sewing the two circles together, you may wish to place something in between them.**

   Herbs, incense, an oil, a small crystal, anything that may help and also reflect your purpose.

7. **Sew around the edges of the circle, binding the front and the back together.**

   The half-inch square now forms a loop through which we can slip a necklace of some sort and wear the talisman around our neck.

The talisman is cut and folded over, to be sewn along the edges of the circle. You may wish to place a dream crystal between the two sides prior to sewing. You now have a talisman to wear.

ANGELILC TALISMAN AFTER FOLD

The Angelic Talisman

8. **It is important to stay focused on the task.**

   Once you start, do not stop until finished. See and feel it coming alive, activating its corresponding archetypal forces. Visualize the symbols as you work on each step; see each symbol awakening energy to help you.

9. **At its completion, perform a small blessing and meditation ritual with it.**

   Smudging it or running it through cleansing incense is even more effective. You may want to put a drop or two of essential oil or flower elixir to amplify its effects. Angelica flower elixir is good for this.

10. **Place the talisman over your head.**

    Feel its energy come alive. Feel the archangelic influence surrounding you and embracing you.

EXERCISE:

Archangels	Associated With
MICHAEL 	Archangel of protection and balance, controls the dragons in our lives, protects against psychic imbalances and tears down the old and intrusive.
GABRIEL 	Archangel of hope and illumination, reveals through dreams, protects against manipulation and anything dealing with sexuality
RAPHAEL 	Archangel of healing and miracles, helps remove obstacles and problems, brings mental clarity
AURIEL 	Archangel of vision, awakens insight into problems and their solutions, protects animals and nature, awakens harmony

The Angelic Talisman

Symbols	Colors	Element	Astrology
spear, dragon	red, fire colors	fire	Ares, Leo, Sagittarius
white rose, turtle	emerald and sea green, black and white	water	Cancer, Scorpio, Pisces
Holy Grail, phoenix	blue and gold	air	Gemini, Libra, Aquarius
weddings, unicorn	silver white, black and yellow	earth	Taurus, Virgo, Capricorn

Chapter 11

Advanced Techniques for Protection

Think of yourself as an incandescent power, illuminated and perhaps forever talked to by God and his messengers.

Brenda Ueland

Many people claim that because they have their visions, their spirit contacts, and understand that all knowledge lies within, there is no reason to use strong protection techniques. The truth is that the knowledge of protection techniques enables us to keep our vision unimpaired, guarding us against dangers we may not be aware of.

It is easy to misuse energies awakened through psychic development or to express them in an unbalanced fashion. Psychic development releases energies which can affect the mind and which can create subtle difficulties if care is not taken. The increased sensitivity alone can easily render anyone suspicious and quarrelsome.

Rather than trying to dominate the universe, we are trying to work within its rhythms. Those who "dabble" with a little bit of knowledge and experience are the ones most likely to find themselves in difficulty.[1]

Contact with non-physical states has a powerful effect upon us as it tends to draw the living from this plane of objective, physical life, which is where we are supposed to be focused. The higher the energies we contact, the more likely this is to occur. This is why careful integration of practice with the physical is so important and why physical health and well-being are so essential for our psychic well-being.

Work with the spiritual and the psychic should never imply neglect of the physical. If the physical is unbalanced, then the expression of the spiritual through us will be also. Stronger protection techniques are necessary for those seeking higher initiation to close the doors strongly behind us and seal them so that we learn to express the energies we have touched in a more balanced fashion.

At times much more intense methods are necessary to cleanse an environment and to protect our energies. We are exposed to so many energies and stimuli that it becomes difficult to discern and distinguish them all. There are things that can be done regularly to help us with these situations and for those situations which are even less pleasant, as in the case of psychic attack.

The exercises described in this chapter are intensely purifying and cleansing and recommended to everyone for overall health and well-being. They are especially encouraged

---

[1] Dabbling is the reading or examining of something superficially and then attempting to teach or perform more in-depth practices for which the person is in reality unprepared. For example, an individual who has read several books on shamanism and tries to present himself or herself as a shaman is dabbling. To become a shaman involves years of training and much dedication and work within a cultural framework.

for anyone working in the psychic and holistic field on any level. They are a part of my daily routine. I think of them as a gift to myself.

I have witnessed the successful use of these exercises in every aspect of psychic protection. I've seen the Banishing Ritual exercise performed in homes where outside individuals have been projecting negative energies (even visiting astrally) upon the residents. As a result, I have seen these same intruders manifest welts, as if they had been spiritually scorched, for their tampering and trespassing when The Banishing Ritual of the Pentagram exercise was performed.

These exercises, The Banishing Ritual of the Pentagram and The Qabalistic Cross,[2] are based upon the ancient Hebrew Qabala, but we do not have to be schooled in the Qabalistic tradition to be able to use them or benefit from them. The audio tape can even be played throughout the day without actual participation to enhance the protective energies.

---

[2] These exercises are available on audio cassette and can be ordered through your local bookstore. For more information, see pages 356-357.

EXERCISE: 𝕿𝖍𝖊 𝕼𝖆𝖇𝖆𝖑𝖎𝖘𝖙𝖎𝖈 𝕮𝖗𝖔𝖘𝖘

BENEFITS:

- stabilizes the aura
- balances, calms, and strengthens our focus

Since the Qabalistic Cross exercise[3] can be used to stabilize the aura and protect us, it should be used before any meditation, pathworking, imagickal technique, and even ritual. It should also be used to close your activity, to help seal off other planes and dimensions, grounding you and the energies you have activated in a balanced manner. With time and practice, through this exercise we become more conscious of the overshadowing presence of our own higher divine genius.

---

[3] This exercise is available on audio cassette and can be ordered through your local bookstore. For more information, see pages 356-357.

1. **Stand straight (or in a seated position), feet together, shoulders back, and arms at your side.**

   Face east, if possible.

2. **Take several deep breaths from the diaphragm.**

   As you inhale and exhale slowly, visualize yourself growing and expanding into the heavens. Do this until you can visualize and imagine yourself standing upon the earth, with the entire universe surrounding you.

3. **With the thumb (spirit), the index finger (fire) and the middle finger (earth) together, touch the forehead between and above the brows. Slowly intone the Hebrew word:**

   Ateh (ah-tOh)

   Give equal emphasis to each syllable, and visualize the sound carrying to the ends of the universe. In English, this translates as "thine is."

4. **Drawing the hand with the joined thumb and fingers downward, as if drawing the light of the universe down and through the body, touch the solar plexus and tone the word:**

   Malkuth (mahl-kUth)

   This means "the kingdom." As you tone the word, imagine the light passing through the body down through the feet, so that you see a column of light that extends from the heavens through you and into the heart of the Earth.

EXERCISE:

5. **Bring the right hand, with the thumb and fingers joined to the right shoulder and tone the words:**

    Ve Geburah (vuh-guh-bU-rah)

    This translates as "the Power." As you tone this, touching the shoulder, see an explosion of light, that releases a stream of crystalline light that extends to infinity to the right.

6. **Move the thumb and fingers from the right shoulder across the body to the left shoulder. As you touch the left shoulder, there is another explosion of light, and you tone the words:**

    Ve Gedulah (vuh-guh-dU-lah)

    This translates as "the glory." As you tone them, a stream of light issues forth, extending to infinity to your left. You now have a vertical stream of light passing through you from the heavens to the Earth. You also have a horizontal stream of light passing through you at shoulder level, extending to infinity.

7. **Raise both arms out to the side, palms upward, and then lay the hands over each other at the heart. Tone strongly the words:**

    Le Olam Amen (leh-O-lahm-ah-mehn)

    This translates as "forever, Amen." As you tone them, see yourself a living, equal-armed cross of light.

The Qabalistic Cross

Enhance this exercise by visualizing a brilliant crystalline white light descending from on high, through our head, down through the feet, and into the heart of the planet. This light extends vertically through the body to infinity in both directions. Then visualize a second shaft of light from shoulder to shoulder, extending in both directions to infinity. As we make the cross of light, touching each of the four designated points on the body, visualize brilliant explosions of light. They should engulf each of the four directions, filling the body and extending into the lines of light.

Vibrate or tone the words strongly and clearly. If need be, tone them several times. This not only improves concentration, but can help us to formulate the cross more clearly and vividly. We want the cross to be so brilliant that it is blinding in its intensity and actually lights up the universe, becoming a living cross of light within the universe and all dimensions.

When visualizing, focus on the idea of divine white brilliance. The vibrations of the words and the visualization attract a certain force to you. The nature and intensity of the force rests largely on the your mind's condition. Thus we want to focus on the highest, most brilliant, and zmost divine.

As we breathe in, breathe in the brilliance. As we slowly emit the breath, we should slowly pronounce the words. See and feel them vibrating and ringing throughout the universe with glory and power. At the end, visualize yourself assuming normal size, absorbing the brilliance into yourself as you return. In this way, it becomes a part of the light for your physical world.

EXERCISE: The Banishing Ritual of the Pentagram

BENEFITS:

- intensely pruifying to self and environments
- very grounding
- cleansing on all levels
- especially effective with negative thoughtforms and psychic attack

---

This simple ritual involves using the power of the divine names associated with the Tree of Life, along with the power of the Archangels, for protective purposes. It is a protection against impure magnetism and influences. It cleanses the aura as well as the environment in which it is performed.

This exercise[4] builds a field of positive, protective, brilliant energy around you and your environment. It can be used to get rid of obsessive thoughts, protect against psychic attack, shield against lower astral entities, dissipate negative thoughtforms, and seal the doors of other dimensions. It can cleanse the aura of negativity accumulated throughout the day

---

[4] This exercise is available on audio cassette and can be obtained through your local store. For more information, see pages 356-357.

by our contact with others, and it seals the home against negativity projected towards it.

This banishing ritual should be practiced by anyone within the metaphysical or spiritual field. Those doing ritual work, those just beginning to open to other energies and dimensions, those in psychic development, and even those in healing work should practice it everyday to build a force field to prevent unwanted intrusions.

This exercise builds a ring of spiritual fire, studded in four directions with five-pointed stars of flame. It prevents anything other than the highest from entering into the environment. The more this technique is used, the more protective it becomes. It will set up a seal around your environment that dissolves negativity before it can reach you or after you have been touched by it.

The banishing ritual prevents a bleed-through of subtle energies from other dimensions. Through it only the highest and truest vibrations can pass through the ring of fire, unless we invite it.

Once it is established, the sphere of sensation is purified, exalted, and made impenetrable to disturbing influences. With such a purified aura, we can go anywhere, do almost anything, visit most other dimensions without a fear of problems or attack. We must realize though that it is not a cure-all for a lack of temperance, patience, or common sense.

NOTE

Initially this should be practiced everyday. It should also be performed at the end of pathworkings or ritual, for sometimes the doors do not close entirely. In time, it builds up permanently within your environment, so that only occasional reinforcement is necessary.

EXERCISE:

1. **Stand, facing East.**

    Perform the Qabalistic cross.

2. **Step forward with the left foot, symbolic of "entering within."**

3   **Using your finger, a dagger, athame, or a lighted stick of incense, draw in the air before you a banishing pentagram.**

    Begin at the left hip and draw a fiery line in the air before you to a point just above your head. See the line as a blue flame. (This is a lot like creating the astral doorways.)

    Without stopping, continue the line down to outside the right hip. From the right hip, draw upward to just outside the left shoulder. Then continue the line of fire across the front of you to the right shoulder.

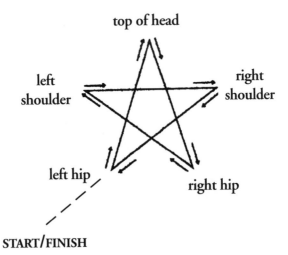

The Banishing Ritual of the Pentagram

From the right shoulder, bring the line back to the left hip, where you started. Envision a fiery blue pentagram in the air before you.

4. **Thrust you finger (dagger, athame, or lighted incense stick) into the heart of that pentagram and tone the divine name:**

Yod He Vau He (yOd-hA-vOv-hA)

Do this slowly and fully. Keep the finger pointing in the center. Visualize and feel the pentagram expand and explode with an intense blue heat and energy, engulfing you, your aura, and all of your surroundings to the East.

Visualize the pentagram continuing to grow, its heat and fire burning out all impurities and cleansing the entire eastern quarter of the world. Then it lodges in the East, burning strong and steady with purity and permanence.

5. **Still holding the arm extended, pointing toward the heart of the pentagram, slowly rotate to the south (a quarter turn to the right).**

As your arm moves with the body, see a stream of fire arc from the pentagram in the East to a point in the south. See this as the beginning of a protective wall or ring of flame. When completed, it will seal you within that ring of purity—sealing out negativity.

EXERCISE:

6. **Drop the hand to a point outside the left hip, and just as you did in the East, inscribe in the air before you a second flaming pentagram in the South. Then thrust your finger into the heart of that pentagram and intone the divine name:**

   Adonai (ah-dOh-nI)

   Visualize the same effects as with the star in the east, only now the South is being purified and cleansed, and the pentagram lodges itself permanently in the South.

   There are now two fiery pentagrams with an arc of flame connecting them.

7. **With finger still extended, rotate another quarter turn to the West. See that arc of flame continuing, now to link the pentagram in the South with a point in the West. Inscribe in the air, a third pentagram, and as you thrust your finger into it, you intone the divine name:**

   Eheieh (A-huh-yAh)

   The pentagram expands, growing, purifying everything to the West.

   You have now established the third pentagram and they are connected with a growing arc of flame.

The Banishing Ritual of the Pentagram

8. **Holding the arm straight out, you turn another quarter turn to the North, so that the arc of flame now extends from the East to the South to the West and to the North. Visualize and inscribe in the air a fourth pentagram of fire. Thrust your finger into the center and intone:**

   Agla[5] (ah-gah-lah)

   As the fourth pentagram expands, it burns and purifies everything to the South.

9. **With arm still extended, rotate to the East, completing the arc of flame and fire.**

   This is the protective ring of fire, studded in the four directions with flaming pentagrams. As you complete the circle, an explosion of purifying fire passes through you, around you—further cleansing and protecting the environment.

   This ring of fire and the pentagrams now burn upon the ethers and within the universe.

10. **Drop your arms as you face the East and breathe deeply of the purified air.**

    See and feel everything around you cleansed and protected. Then, still facing East, extend your arms out to your side, palms upward, and speak the words:

    Before me, Raphael!

---

[5] This is not a divine name like the others, but an abbreviation for the words *Ateh Gedulah le-Olam Adonai.* This translates as "Thou are mighty forever, O Lord."

EXERCISE:

Intone the name of the archangel strongly and clearly. Visualize a column of blue and gold light forming before you.

From this column of light steps a powerful being whose energy seems to fan the air around you. You feel a rush of air which revitalizes the aura. It is contact with great healing and protection.

This being nods to you and then faces away from you, to protect you against any intrusion into your space—to guard the East for you.

11. With arms still outstretched, you intone the words:

Behind me, Gabriel!

Visualize a column of emerald green light forming behind you.

From it steps a figure of those same colors with flashes of light. This being is electrical in nature, and you can feel it.

This is Gabriel, a battery to the universe, and from this being comes the basis of all vision. The figure nods to you and then turns to face away from you to guard the West for you.

12. With arms still outstretched, you intone the words:

On my right hand, Michael!

To your right a column of crystalline red light begins to appear, blazing with all the reds of fire.

The Banishing Ritual of the Pentagram

From it steps a magnificent being, sword upraised. This great archangel handles and purges the unbalanced forces of nature.

This being nods to you and then turns away from you to face and guard the South for you.

13. Then tone the words:

On my left hand, Auriel!

Visualize a column of crystalline white.

From that column of light there steps a giant figure. This being has the primeval light of the Divine and works to manifest it upon the Earth. This being works with the light of all teachings.

This magnificent being nods to you and then turns away, facing outward to guard the North for you.

14. Visualize all of the archangels surrounding you within this ring of fire. Feel their protection, their energies and blessings. Then speak clearly the words:

Before me flame the pentagrams!
In the column of Light that I AM
shines the six-rayed star![6]

Visualize a six-pointed star shining with brilliance in the heart.

---

[6] "In the column of light" refers to the light of the physical body, the column of light you became through the Qabalistic cross.

EXERCISE:

15. Visualize and feel the entire scene.

Then seal it all into place by performing the Qabalistic cross once more. It locks the protection upon the ethers for you.

In this exercise, the archangels face away from us to guard against anything false, unhealthy, unbalanced, impure, or negative. We are encircled by them—within a ring of fire, studded with flaming pentagrams. We are sealed in with blessing, balance, strength, and health!

The Banishing Ritual of the Pentagram

From the best selling books:
HOW TO SEE AND READ THE AURA
SIMPLIFIED MAGIC

Psychic Protection

Ted Andrews

PSYCHIC PROTECTION
This audio cassette contains The Middle Pillar of Light and
The Banishing Ritual of the Pentagram
(including The Qabalistic Cross).
With this tape you hear the pronunciations
of the divine force names as you perform the exercise.

PSYCHIC PROTECTION   by Ted Andrews   275

PART III: WALKING THE SPIRITUAL PATH

Part III:

Walking the Spiritual Path

Such gardens are not made by singing,
"Oh, how beautiful," and sitting in the shade.

Rudyard Kipling

Chapter 12

Spiritual Responsibility and Initiation

In heaven, learning is seeing;
on earth, it is remembering.
Happy is he who has gone through the Mysteries;
he knows the source and end of life.

Pindar

For anyone involved in anything with the psychic realm, practice and training are essential. Without it there is little control. In the beginning, all psychic energy can be very strong and unbalancing until we learn to turn it on and off at will.

As we have discussed frequently throughout this book, fear and anxiety are the greatest obstacles in the development of our own psychic sensitivities and in protecting ourselves. As much as possible, we should always guard against cluttering the mind with negative emotions.

We should approach the entire realm with cautious optimism. Groups provide some wonderful advantages. Mostly, they provide a safe, protected, and hopefully, an encouraging climate for development and exploration of the psychic realm. Remember though that there might arise a time to move beyond the group. We must learn to use our abilities outside of the group environment or our abilities may become intermittent and less reliable.

As we open to the psychic realm, some wonderful blessings and opportunities occur, but we should not be too eager to step out and demonstrate newly developed abilities. Until control is truly developed, it is easy to exhaust ourselves. Control is always the key to effective development and protection—and to continual spiritual growth.

Control the Key to Spiritual Growth

Control is often a problem with many old time psychics and mediums. They stay tuned into everyone and everything they encounter, afraid to shut down. They often fear that if they shut down their sensitivities, they may not be able to turn them on again. This is a fallacy, and it is extremely unhealthy. We can learn to turn our sensitivities and abilities on and off at will. It takes time and practice.

Most of us at some point have or will experience mediums and psychics who look as if they have been run through a wringer. They are tired and ill. Their health is often poor, which should cause us to question their abilities. Psychic information must be translated through the medium of the body. If our body is out of balance, it is likely that the information will be as well.

Individuals who truly develop and control their intuitive faculties are strong and vibrant. No matter what age they are, there is a strong vitality about them. These individuals have gained positive control over their faculties. They do not allow it to function without their conscious permission (except in exceptional cases), and they are able to use it to some degree under all circumstances and conditions. These are the psychics who never use their abilities without regard for limits of time, moral obligations, and their own physical capabilities. Unfortunately, many spiritual and "New Age" aspirants attempt to BE before they have learned to BECOME. This will always trip them up through a variety of imbalances.

There is an old Qabalistic adage: "A vision of God is not the same as seeing God face to face." In other words, a vision is not a promise of what will be. It is a reflection of what can be if there is the proper preparation, knowledge, and application of focus, energy, and persistence.

Knowledge is ineffective unless it can be applied and integrated into one's life and essence in a balanced and creative manner. When we integrate our knowledge, it brings understanding and wisdom. True wisdom is the proper application of knowledge and understanding to life.

Our mind is a gateway to other dimensions. It has been said that we enter the mysteries through the sphere of the mind, but only so we can worship at the shrine in the heart. Humans have grown increasingly rational in their thinking processes during this past century, and often this colors our higher feelings. Today we need to link the mind with the heart—creating within ourselves intelligence of the heart.

The true spiritual student should be familiar with the spiritual investigations and philosophies of the past. There must be the ability for complete and independent testing of the knowledge. The individual needs to develop the ability to draw correspondences and see relationships—similar and dissimilar. He or she must be able to discern the truth from half-truth and illusions from reality.

Knowledge can upset all previous conditions of the mind and body. Through higher spiritual knowledge, we learn that there is often as much to unlearn as there is to learn. Any lack of control of the knowledge we acquire and how we apply it has the potential to disrupt and unbalance lives, with repercussions on all levels of our being. There are no short-cuts. We must learn to open to higher knowledge and to use it to integrate the spiritual forces surrounding us into our daily lives in a balanced fashion.

This doesn't mean it will be easy. It just means that now we have a great tool to help us so we can learn to invoke and invite energies into our lives that can bring results. This requires great time and effort, but it also brings great rewards.

The first lesson of knowledge is that nothing is insignificant. Everything has importance and consequence within our lives, helping to shape us. Learning to utilize and incorporate all of our energies at all times—in full consciousness and with

Chinese Sorcerers

full responsibility—is the Great Work. It is BECOMING more than human; it is what makes us a human BEING.

Three Tests of Higher Initiation

Today we often hear the term "ascension" being bandied about in metaphysical groups and gatherings. It is just another word for higher initiation, and the process, no matter what it is termed, is still the same. Each must still win for himself or herself the conditions for higher initiation and heightened consciousness, though some wish to believe ascension involves a higher force taking everyone beyond the mundane into a realm in which troubles and difficulties are dissolved.

The modern initiate must be able to take the knowledge, instructions, and meditative content of his or her life, judge all of these pieces independently, and then decide what specific steps in esoteric learning can be applied to his or her individual development. If unable to carry through this necessary self-observation, judgment, and the obligation it is based upon, then more preparation is needed.

The process begins by being able to recognize the devine spark is within you and that ultimately no one knows better for you than you. Yes, we all need teachers at times to guide us and help us connect more fully with that divine spark, but regardless of credentials, titles, degrees, or abilities, the decisions concerning your life and the ensuing responsibilities and consequences are yours alone! This demands the development of steadfast perception and cognition—in both the physical world and the supersensible realms as well. This requires careful self-observation, discrimination, and judgment, and great control of our own spiritual processes.

Everyone who intends to work for heightened consciousness and initiation will be tested along three avenues:
**discrimination, the test of the teacher, and uncontrolled
fancy.**

DISCRIMINATION

The test of discrimination is the first thing we encounter and the last thing we will be tested upon on the spiritual
path. We must be able to discriminate and discern reality from
illusion, the false from the true, when to act, how best to act,
where to focus our energies, when not to focus, whom to
believe and whom not to believe. We each must be able to
determine half-truths.

In the ancient Qabalistic Tree of Life, discrimination is
the test associated with the level of consciousness known as
Malkuth, at the base of the Tree of Life. Thus discrimination
must be the basis of all our studies in the physical and
non-physical world.

Connecting with supersensible states of consciousness
and those beings and energies existing within them does not
make us omniscient or omnipotent. It demands even greater
testing and discernment because those realms are more fluid,
changeable, and unfamiliar. The expressions of energy in the
more subtle realms of life span the spectrum of positive and
negative—as greatly as our own physical world.

TEST OF THE TEACHER

This is the testing of our ability to discern complete and
truthful teachings and to recognize their sources. Today there
are many that express a knowledge of how to work with the
more subtle energies of life, but it does not mean that the
methods are necessarily appropriate or beneficially creative,

THE QABALISTIC TREE OF LIFE

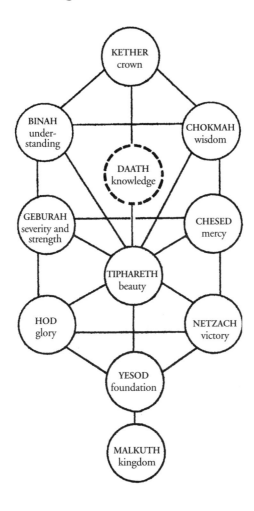

regardless of the momentary effectiveness. I have met a great number of individuals who have read a book or two and immediately set themselves up as a teacher.

Any time greater knowledge becomes more accessible, there is the opportunity to use it for greater benefit. There is also ample opportunity for it to be misused, sometimes consciously and sometimes unknowingly. Test and discriminate what comes to you, whether through a book or a person. Remember that no one knows better for you than YOU.

Chapter 13 provides a number of questions that you can ask yourself when talking with other psychics and those who channel information. It also provides information on ways to observe their lifestyle and behavior, not so that you will become critical of others, but rather so you will learn to discern true teachings from false teachings. When we are able to do this, then our teachers and the teaching we encounter become mediators and assistants for our own bridge building to higher consciousness.

UNCONTROLLED FANCY

This is the test of our ability to discern the maya and illusions that affect us when we begin to open to the more ethereal realms. Visions, channelings, and insights can be nothing more than uncontrolled fancy, a manifestation of our own imaginings to stroke the ego. What may come through as spiritual insight may be little more than a fanciful manufacturing to verify what we already know or to justify our viewpoint.

Imagination is important to unfolding our higher potential, but it must be controlled. Sometimes the difference is difficult to detect, which is why continual self-observation is essential in all of the spiritual practices. Not delving deeply enough, accepting blindly, and failing to be objective can all lead to uncontrolled fancy.

Self-Observation and Personal Reflection

Today more than ever there is a much greater need to test and validate all of our experiences. The difficulty for most people is figuring out how. There are not always clear signals. The techniques and information presented throughout this book should lay a strong foundation. Sometimes though, the determining is trial and error, but even that helps us to learn and grow.

Always begin with some simple questions about our experiences:

1. Did the experience help us (all parties involved) to resolve situations?

2. Did the experience make us more productive and creative in all areas of our life?

3. Does the experience or teaching have practical applications within our life?

4. Does the teaching blend the rational with the intuitive, the practical with the imaginative, the scientific with the philosophical, and the physical with the spiritual?

If our experiences accomplish these things, then we are truly opening to higher initiation. We are on the right path.

When this occurs, there arise many benefits. Our health improves and we experience more vitality and vibrancy.

We have less stress and handle the stress we do have more effectively and creatively. Our decisionmaking ability improves, and we generally have more control over all aspects of our life. Creativity and inspiration boom within our lives, opening new doors and potentials. We become relaxed but energized, and we have a much larger perspective on life and all of its various situations.

As we open more fully to the subtle realms of life, our lives are blessed. Our intuition unfolds and increases, and our childlike wonder at life returns and grows. We remember what we always knew within our hearts—that we could starve as much from a lack of wonder as from a lack of food.

The Quest for The Holy Grail

Modern Spiritual Initiation

It is the destiny of humans to conquer matter. This is the quest for the spirit, a search for our innermost part, the point of our greatest reality. It is not a path up to some divine light from which there is no return. Neither is it a path in which our problems and trials are dissolved in a blinding light of spirituality. It is our destiny to bring out the spirit into matter. That is when "the kingdom of heaven" manifests. Part of our life duty is to spiritualize matter, not to escape from it. The spiritual path is the search for a way to bring the spiritual aspects of life into our daily existence.

All of the ancient teachings and scriptures use similar terms to describe this magickal process. Gateways, doors, the outer court, the inner court, temple, the Holy of Holies, the quest, the pilgrimage, and many other words and terms are part of the ancient mystery language that hinted at and veiled the teachings that could assist the individual in manifesting a higher destiny, a more magickal existence. This mystery language often related to stages of development and training, reflecting the unfolding of our spirituality into our daily life.

Every civilization and religion has had its magickal teachings, its spiritual *Mysteries*. The phraseology may have changed and differed, but only to conform to the needs of the time and place.

> What is extraordinary, however, is that there are more similarities than differences in the methods used by the secret traditions to change the consciousness of their respective practitioners.[1]

---

[1] Gaeton Delaforge, *The Templar Tradition* (Putney, VT: Threshold Books, 1987), p. 3.

Today the mystical and magickal teachings are still called Mysteries, as they have been called for eons. In more ancient times, the Mystery teachings of life were zealously guarded against outside intrusion to prevent their profaning, which draws the attention of the masses and fuels superstitions, fears, and narrow-mindedness about anything occult.

In the Western world, this unfoldment of the Mysteries is most often referred to as "The Quest for the Holy Grail." This quest serves two purposes for the modern spiritual student:

1. It is the search to discover and to awaken our true spiritual essence, our innermost self with all of its potentials, and

2. It is the quest for the best manner in which to express our highest potentials, abilities, and essence within this life.

The potential to accelerate and awaken our own divinity is within our ability. It is for this reason that above the portals of the ancient mystery schools was the phrase KNOW THYSELF! This is the first stage of training in any true system of magick and spirituality. It requires an impersonal approach to all of our desires and beliefs we have feared facing—not always a pleasant task. It often involves purging and stripping away the veils of pretense—those we have placed upon ourselves and those we have allowed society to place upon us.

This process is often repeated and frequently requires we retreat from time to time from active study and exploration, but we always return stronger and further along the path than we would have been had we continued to force the growth. In many ways it is similar to the stripping process we go through at death, but only when it occurs while still fulfilling our life obligations in a creative and positive manner do we progress the most.

We can be our own worst enemy in this process. We either can't or won't make the most of our opportunities, refusing to deal with our obligations and our hardships in a creative manner. We may resort to quick methods that ultimately create tremendously damaging difficulties down the road. These can vary from emotional imbalances to misuse of one's energies by others or use that can hinder the progress of others, preventing them from becoming channels of light. Many just halt because the process is too great or demands too much effort. There are NO shortcuts to true spirituality. The path of metaphysics and magick is never quick and easy.

There exists a major misconception today concerning the spiritual path and higher initiation. Many assume wrongly that if they are not actively working in the field of metaphysics (new age, magic, mysticism, psychicism), they cannot truly be making progress. If not ostensibly demonstrating psychic ability or learnings, they wrongly assume they are not growing. As a result, there is a preponderance of individuals trying to teach and work in this new economic market place without the depth of knowledge and experience to do so in the safest and most beneficial manner for all.

Often it is a matter of ego, a way for individuals to tell others of their "specialness." It is a way for many to make themselves stand out as unique. Yes, there are many highly qualified individuals in this field, but there are also a tremendous number who are unqualified. The unfortunate part is that the average person entering into this realm is rarely capable of discerning the good from the bad.

It was to prevent such things that the ancient mystery schools required an active life aside from the spiritual studies and work. It is also why many such schools required silence in the first two (and sometimes ten) years of study. They recognized that through the fulfillment of daily obligations in a creative manner we are propelled along our spiritual path.

It is not the demonstration of psychic ability or healing or book learning that unfolds our greatest potential. In fact, quite often such demonstrations can hinder our growth, especially in the early years of training. Rather than concentrating and focusing the transformative energy accessed in the learning process, the energy is dissipated by using it to teach or do psychic work prematurely. The need or desire to be out front, displaying, is part of what ultimately must be purged.

Yes, when we begin to open to these dynamic forces, it is wonderful and only natural to want to share with others. Opening to these universal energies is inspiring and will stimulate a great desire to share the illumination with others, but there is a proper time and place—one that is beneficial for you and for those with whom you share. Sharing the experience prematurely can dissipate its power and ability to work for you most effectively. The teaching opportunities will present themselves and evolve naturally in their own time—always a signal that we are on the right path and doing the right thing.

Not everyone will be open to your sharing. The raised eyebrows of others can create blocks and raise your own doubts, slowing your progress. Ultimately, it is through the daily trials and tests that we begin to unfold our sleeping potential, enabling ourselves to identify and then lay down outworn patterns so that the newer can come through.

For most people, this will involve simply opening the hearts of those they touch on a daily basis through a smile, a kind word, or the meeting of an obligation or responsibility. Such individuals may not be demonstrating their knowledge or acquiring the attention so many others seem to receive, but this does not mean they are less evolved.

This is the Quest for the Holy Grail, and for each person it is different. For some, the form of the quest will involve working and teaching in the metaphysical field as we know it today. For others, it will take the form of simply living their daily lives in a creative manner and being a positive influence in the lives of those they touch. Unfortunately, not all have the wisdom or patience to see this.

The form of our life quest does not matter because the secret of all holy quests is that ALL who go forth in whatever manner will succeed! Through our quest, we will discover that we are never given a hope, wish, or dream without also being given opportunities to make them a reality!

Chapter 13

Discernment and Testing

Whenever I have to choose between two evils,
I always like to try the one I haven't tried before.

Mae West

Whenever I did psychic readings out of town or state,
it was my custom to seek out the addresses and
phone numbers of various social service agencies
for that area. Having done readings for many years, I was well
aware that many consultations have little to do with psychic
information.

About ten years ago I was participating in a psychic fair
and expo. Aside from doing some lectures, I was also doing
some mini-readings (15-minute psychic readings) more for
entertainment and promotional purposes than anything else.
My first client of the day was a woman who was extremely
distraught and suicidal. Her husband had recently left her
because his ex-wife had committed suicide, and he blamed
himself.

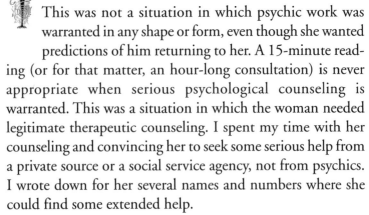

This was not a situation in which psychic work was warranted in any shape or form, even though she wanted predictions of him returning to her. A 15-minute reading (or for that matter, an hour-long consultation) is never appropriate when serious psychological counseling is warranted. This was a situation in which the woman needed legitimate therapeutic counseling. I spent my time with her counseling and convincing her to seek some serious help from a private source or a social service agency, not from psychics. I wrote down for her several names and numbers where she could find some extended help.

The sad part is that I have seen others in situations like this. All too often, the psychics try to handle it themselves. Most psychics have little training for such affairs, and although their hearts may be in the right place, their actions are often inappropriate and can be quite damaging. If any psychic work is done in this type of situation, it should be to assess how best to help and direct the client.

A lack of well-rounded training and development can be damaging to us on so many levels whether we are working professionally with psychic work or not. Even if only exploring our inner potentials for our own private purposes, there are many considerations, many lessons involving balance, health, responsibility, and protection for ourselves and those we may touch in some way.

Awakening Our
True Spiritual Essence

There are many responsibilities upon the spiritual path. In more ancient times, a master or a teacher oversaw the awakening to higher levels of consciousness and aligning them with day-to-day consciousness. The ancients recognized that opening to higher planes and more subtle energies would stimulate what in the East are called *siddhis*, or psychic energies. When activated, these energies will require balancing and proper expression on a daily basis. They require great experience in handling them responsibly.

The siddhis are the energies of our true spiritual essence. They work through our lives whether we are aware of them or not. They bind and flow through our subtle body into our physical lives, all from our spiritual essence or higher self. When stimulated or awakened more fully through study, spiritual and occult exploration, meditation, dynamic prayer, psychic development, and a myriad of other ways, our spiritual essence becomes more closely aligned with our physical being. This releases greater amounts of its creative force into our lives, affecting us physically, emotionally, mentally, and spiritually.

Through psychic development and spiritual studies, we try to bridge our spiritual essence to our physical being, so we can access it consciously at any time we desire for any purpose. When we make efforts to "raise our consciousness," we stimulate the release of energy from our spiritual essence to be expressed within the physical life. When we undertake psychic development in any form, there will always be an increased flow of creative forces that will manifest in our lives, with the potential of affecting all levels of our being and all areas of our life.

Expressing Our Spiritual Energy

Ancient masters and teachers knew that concentrated study in the spiritual sciences and the leading of a spiritually disciplined life possessed greater potential for releasing creative forces more tangibly into the physical life. This energy, once released, must find expression. That expression can be either beneficial or detrimental because energy is neutral, neither good nor evil. It is only our expression and use of energy that determines its degree of goodness. That expression may become disruptive and destructive, finding inappropriate outlets in the physical life if there is not proper mental, emotional, and moral foundations. It will overstimulate the individual in a variety of ways, affecting our physical, emotional, and mental health and balance. If not prepared for, it will often find outlet through the person's own weaknesses, augmenting them, and bringing them out into the open.

One of the more common expressions is through an increase in sexual energy, a physical manifestation and reflection of a tronger and more awakened creative life force. This is a physical response informing us that our creative, psychic energies are being stimulated.

Deciding Which Path to Follow

There are always certain things best not to meddle with. We should never try to dominate nature, but rather work with its rhythms. We should never try to bind, control, and dominate the spirit beings or human beings. We should never intrude upon the free will and creativity of others.

Those who dabble with a little bit of knowledge and experience and believe they can handle it all are the ones most likely to find themselves in difficulty. It is usually those who play and seek psychic thrills under the guise of growing and experimenting, often ending end up in trouble. The psychic world can be deceptive because it is not always bound by the natural laws of the physical world. Because of this, it can mislead those who are not truly trained into activities and delusions that are dangerous.

A psychic is always sensitive, and troubles from hypersensitivity can arise. Most often these problems occur through improper methods of training or training under unsuitable conditions. If we form rapport with other beings and dimensions without the knowledge of how to break the connections and reseal the aura, it can bring out psychic and mental pathologies. This often results at some point in a dissociation of the personality and a variety of other disorders.

The difference between white and black occultism and right- and left-hand paths is not as easy to define as many may believe.

THE RIGHT-HAND PATH

The right-hand path always prolongs the line of evolution, leading by the most direct route to its goal. It always involves measuring actions against the current of evolution. Among the Native Americans, for example, decisions were frequently not made or actions taken until the effects were examined on the next seven generations. The individual on the right-hand path is centered always on the Divine.

THE LEFT-HAND PATH

The left-hand path is the one in which individuals ally themselves consciously with evil. We must keep in mind though that evil is frequently different things to different people. It is essentially ignorance and imbalance. Some individuals stray upon the left-hand path unintentionally or are manipulated onto it. (See also the "Group Mind and Manipulation" section in Chapter 4.)

Those consciously working upon the left-hand path are always self-centered rather than Divine centered. Greed, lust, and a desire for knowledge and power for their own sake motivate them. These individuals usually seek to open psychic faculties by speedier and less troublesome means. (Drugs are often a part of this, but drugs do not allow control and can result in dangerous astral contacts.)

The left-hand path often involves misplaced force and out-of-date methods. There is the misuse of sex under the guise of "spiritual magnetism." It is not unusual to find a generation and expression of the sex force with no self-control or sublimation. Karmic links and associations are created to falsely influence others. There may be abuse of hypnotism and altered states of consciousness for purposes other than the good of the individual.

The left-hand path can be used to open the student to subtler dimensions, but it does not enable the student with any conscious control in those dimensions. Those who are under the influence of a negative or unbalanced occultist will find it difficult to express individuality and will have trouble breaking away.

Choosing Our Path

There is no set code that can be applied to the infinite variety of tests on any path to higher consciousness. Regardless of the path we are on, one of the tests that everyone will encounter time and again is the test of discrimination. There are many forms in which that test may surface, but a common one for everybody at some point is the choice of a teacher and the influence that we allow them to exert upon us.

The influence of the teacher is not through the material presented, as that is available in many forms and is relatively the same everywhere. Rather, the influence occurs through the quality and quantity of energy coming through the teacher in the delivery of the material. The mental link and influence upon students occurs through the increase of energy. This in turn allows greater insight into the material and necessitates greater responsibility on all levels with all individuals in the material's use.

Taking responsibility for our own growth means we open ourselves to greater awareness of life operating on all levels and dimensions. There are many philosophies, ideologies, and teachers to assist us with this. We do not have to limit ourselves to just one. We can gain something from them all.

Any teacher who attempts to tie you to only his or her teachings and methods is on the wrong path, regardless of the knowledge he or she is capable of disseminating. Caution and watchfulness must be exerted at all times, especially if knowledge is dangled like a carrot before us. Remember, knowledge is available to everyone willing to seek it out. There is no one teacher who has sole access to this knowledge regardless of what he or she may say.

Being responsible means that we take whatever we can find from whatever source it appears and we extract it, shape it, and then synthesize it into a system of perpetual growth that works for us as individuals. We use what we learn in the manner best for us, recognizing there is no one doing anything we also can't do in our own unique way. If we remember this, we will never have problems determining whether we are working with right- or left-hand paths or black and white occultism.

Going It Alone

Because of the amount of information and knowledge available today, we do not always need a teacher to open to the more subtle realms of life. Methods and means of doing so can be found everywhere. The problem lies in assuming that the knowledge and information is true and safe. There is a great abundance of information, but much of it is very irresponsible, and so the spiritual student must be even more discerning and discriminating. This is the lesson of spiritual discrimination. It is the first thing we must learn and the last thing we will be tested upon on the spiritual path.

Because of the predominance of information, most people will not align themselves with truly qualified teachers, and this more solitary approach requires even greater personal responsibility. The student of the Mysteries must still earn the conditions necessary for higher initiation and consciousness.

This requires even greater time, care, and attention to the development process.

Today, the spiritual path demands a *fully* conscious union with the spiritually creative worlds. This union cannot be accomplished by mere clairvoyance or psychic insight of any kind. Today's path to manifesting a higher destiny requires a genuine search and use of knowledge and truth. It requires a greater depth of study of all spiritual sciences, remembering that information is not always beneficial and knowledge does not always lead to the truth.

What is psychic is not always spiritual. What is occult is not always beneficial. What is desired is not always uplifting or useful. If we are to truly take control of our spiritual development, we must learn to protect ourselves from all of the psychic junk and pseudo-psychics.

Distinguishing Psychic Junk

Every day on TV, in magazines, and in newspapers there are ads for psychic consultations. For anywhere from three to six dollars a minute, we can have our fortune told. We can learn who our true loves are and how to attain our wealth from "master psychics."

A half-hour consultation on most psychic phone lines can cost as much, if not more, than $150 dollars. Sure, some offer up to "ten free minutes" in their ads, but the ten free minutes must be distributed over five or more calls, which ultimately will cost the client hundreds of dollars with no way of determining the legitimacy of the psychic or the sponsoring company. Plus, there are no guarantees.

An increasing number of professional psychics are working for the psychic phone lines. Some because they do not have to really prove themselves; they can remain anonymous. On the other hand, some do the phone lines because it enables them to work out of their home. Yes, some of phone lines test their professionals to determine their level of ability, but these companies often refuse to provide what their testing procedures are. Tests for psychic abilities have no consistent standard.

I am not saying that all psychics who work the phone lines are ill prepared, but I am saying that it is more difficult to determine a legitimate phone psychic. It is always easier to determine legitimacy person to person, face to face.

Keep in mind too that an individual may be psychic, but that does not necessarily mean they are capable of dispensing advice appropriately. All professional psychics should have some counseling training and experience that can be proven.

Most of the psychic junk (whether in ads or in actual consultations) can be distinguished by certain characteristics. By examining them more closely, we can determine a great deal about the legitimacy of a psychic.

WARNING SIGNALS TO PSEUDO-PSYCHIC WORK

1. Promises to solve all problems.

2. Promises true love.

3. Promises to change your future through magic and spells.

4. Charges exorbitant fees.

5. Does not provide references or legitimate training.

6. Speak only in vague generalities.

7. Focus strongly on death and doom.

8. Promotes frequent appointments.

9. Asks you to do the interpreting.

10. Does little more than stroke your ego.

11. Demands and expects automatic acceptance.

12. Psychic's own life is unhealthy and chaotic.

1. Does the psychic promise or imply a solution to all of your problems?

No psychic is God and will be able to solve all of your problems. A psychic cannot direct your future. He or she can show you options, greater probabilities, but nothing is written in stone because we always have free will. Theoretically, we can change our future by taking a bus rather than driving to work.

A good psychic is able to see patterns within an individual's life and can reveal those patterns to the client, along with the probable outcomes if the patterns are continued. Since most humans rarely change their patterns—even if they know what they are—a high level of accurate predictability is the result.

2. Does the psychic promise to find your true love?

A good psychic will help you to see the ups and downs, the good and the bad of any relationship. If the psychic only talks in glowing terms without speaking of possible problems, then the warning bells should go off. The psychic is more than likely playing to your emotions and to what you wish to hear rather than what actually is.

3. Does the psychic promise to help you change the future through magic and spells?

This is almost always a rip off. Even in today's modern world there are those who wish to blame their troubles on someone's casting spells upon them. Psychics who promise to remove your bad luck through their own spells are going to take advantage of you. They play upon your fears and your misplaced sense of blame. Most people's bad luck is due to bad judgments, not bad spells.

If they promise to cast some spells to increase money and good luck for you, it is a pretty safe bet they will ask you for some money before they do it. The money and good luck is then theirs—not yours. When this happens, offer them a small percentage of the windfall from their spell when it works and not before. And watch how they respond.

4. Does the psychic require that you spend more than $30 for a half hour reading?

Do the math. If it is a psychic phone line, what will 10 minutes cost you? If it is $5 per minute, 10 minutes alone will cost you $50 dollars. Very good and legitimate psychics are going to be reasonably priced. Most legitimate workers in the holistic and psychic field charge frees usually ranging from $20-$100 for up to an hour of their time.

Be wary of exorbitant prices. Although some believe that higher fees indicate a higher quality psychic, it is not necessarily so. When I did private consultations, at my highest price,

I charged only $30 for a half-hour consultation. And I never charged for any healing work because I made my money and paid my bills through teaching. Healing was a way of giving back to the universe. I did require that the healing clients make some donation to a charity of their choice, treat themselves to something special, or do a favor anonymously for another.

5. Does the psychic have legitimate training and references?

Be wary of individuals who advertise themselves as "master psychics" or those who claim certification through some national psychic organization: JOHN DOE IS A MASTER PSYCHIC CERTIFIED THROUGH THE NATIONAL ALLIANCE OF PROFESSIONAL PSYCHICS AND HEALERS.[1]

Although such statements make the individual sound responsible and legitimate, there are very few truly national organizations which control and monitor psychic work. Many of these organizations have created their title as a way of influencing the public with their advertising.

There is no common standard in professional psychic counseling, and titles such as "master psychic" or "avatar" and a myriad of other labels are nothing more than advertising ploys.

When we seek a psychic, we are seeking a service and because of this, we have a right to know something about the psychic. How long has he or she been working as a psychic? What is the psychic's educational background? (We do not have

[1] This is a pseudo-organization whose name I made up to illustrate what is often found in ads and promotions. To my knowledge there is no such organization.

to be highly educated to be psychically developed, but
the more education one has, the better he or she is able
to express and clarify the psychic information to us.)
Does the psychic have any formal counseling training?

Can the psychic provide references? Are there stores,
centers, and individuals who are familiar with the psychic's
work? Most major cities have metaphysical bookstores and
centers, and they can be an invaluable aid in determining the
quality of the psychic.

Attend psychic fairs and holistic expos in your area. Yes,
a lot of psychic fairs are training grounds for beginning
psychics, but such events also draw the more developed as well.
Listen to what people (especially friends) say about the different psychics. Are there some to whom you feel more drawn?
(Yes, it is O.K. to use your own intuition to help you decide.)

Since most psychic fairs offer mini-readings (consultations that are shorter and less expensive), you can visit several
psychics. Compare. Who were you more comfortable with?
Who was more specific and accurate? By visiting several in this
type of setting, we also eliminate a lot of our own fears and
confusions, and when we finally choose a psychic for a full
consultation, we will be more at ease, understand more of what
to expect, and know what to ask.

6. Does the psychic speak in vague generalities?

It is true that some psychics will sometimes relay
messages that can be true for many people. While a lot of the
statements by a psychic may seem to an outsider to be
general, such statements may seem very specific to the client.
The generality is often relative to the individual.

Keeping that in mind, the psychic should be specific at some point during the consultation, providing specific information with a good blend of generalities and details of the past, present, and possible future. Of course, there will always be some clear hits and misses, but there should always be more hits. A good professional psychic should be correct at least 75 to 80 percent of the time.

When I did my private consultations, I always started generally. I would start by reading the aura, speaking of the basic colors and their general meaning to the life of the individual. By the time I finished speaking of the aura, I was well tuned-in to the individual, and then got into specifics.

7. Does the psychic focus on death and doom?

When leaving a psychic reading, we should always feel energized and positive. If we do not, then something was wrong with the consultation. Even if we sought out the psychic for some perspective on serious problems within our life, we should leave with a sense of hope and a sense of knowing there are always possibilities and choices available to us.

Be very wary of psychics who predict death! IF A PSYCHIC PREDICTS YOUR DEATH OR THE DEATH OF SOMEONE CLOSE TO YOU, GET UP AND LEAVE! (I know I am very likely to get mail on this part, so please read the following paragraphs carefully.)

Predictions and statements of death can sow seeds that will hurt and send out energy which can make someone's final days less peaceful for the soul. It can even bring on the death conditions prematurely through stimulating fear and worry. The psychic must always weigh the benefit of statements like these, and all too often such statements are made irresponsibly.

Great caution and responsible behavior is always warranted in these situations. Psychics are never 100 percent correct, and maybe what the psychic experiences is a symbolic death—a transition of some other kind.

Yes, there are times, just before the transition, where it may be readily apparent, but the soul always has free will and much greater strength than is often believed. The psychic has a responsibility to the soul preparing for transition from life, and the only one who ultimately knows when an individual is about to pass on is the individual's soul. It is almost always irresponsible to make such prognostications.

Some people go to psychics to find out information about loved ones who are ill and may be getting ready to die, and their motives are not always honorable.[2] A good psychic should try to determine the honorableness of the client. Even when the motives are honorable, caution should always be used. The client should know there is hope and free will, so as not to sow seeds of fear and worry that can facilitate the premature hastening of death. (Only good counseling training and education will help the psychic do this effectively.)

If you leave a psychic consultation feeling drained, worried, filled with fear—with no more hope and perspective than you went in—it is a good indication that the reading was poor. Good psychic consultations help to stimulate our creative aspects and provide inspiration and hope for becoming more productive within our life circumstances.

---

[2] Individuals who go from psychic to psychic are often referred to as reader hoppers. They are not seeking growth as much as a rush of energy and often some good gossip on others in their life. Most professional psychics should not tune into others without their permission. As a general rule, I never did it except when it involved a child (not an adult age) or in the case of an illness of an immediate family member.

8. Does the psychic recommend frequent, even weekly appointments?

So often I hear of people visiting a psychic every week, once a month, or with a frequency that is completely unwarranted. If a person needs that many sessions, he or she should be seeing a licensed therapeutic professional—not a psychic.

I never did a full consultation more often than once a year. There is rarely enough change to warrant repeated sessions during a 12-month period. When I was doing private work, I always told my clients they could give me a call to set up another appointment 10 to 12 months down the road. In the mean time, if something came up, they could give me a quick phone call. Otherwise, unless it was an extreme situation, there would be no need for any more sessions.

A psychic who encourages repeated sessions is milking the client for reasons other than professional ones. Some psychics are afraid that if they don't do frequent readings, their client will go somewhere else, and so they give in—afraid that there aren't enough clients to go around. This reflects an underlying belief that there is not enough abundance in the world for everyone.

A client who encourages and seeks frequent sessions is not taking responsibility for his or her life.

9. **Does the psychic ask you to do the interpreting for them?**

A good psychic will not only pick up information, sometimes quite symbolic, but also tell you what it means rather than asking you for its meaning. So often I have heard psychics say to clients, "I see a cloud (or any other symbol); does that mean anything to you?"

The psychic should not be asking you the meaning of his or her psychic impressions. Good psychics will have a strong background in working with symbols and images. They should be able to describe them and explain clearly what they mean and how they most likely apply to you.

Yes, all psychics will ask a few questions in the course of a consultation, but most of the time should be spent telling you information and making sure you understand what it all means. Only in this way are you able to know the validity of the psychic. Reputable psychics will not undertake fact finding about you or use information derived from friends or family. They will be able to provide details specific enough to let you know the information is not coming from their questions of you, your body language, or a source other than their own psychic ability.

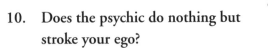

10. Does the psychic do nothing but stroke your ego?

Psychics who only speak of the positive, of only glowing things in your life, are just stroking your ego. They may also be simply picking up on what you wish to hear.

Be wary of psychics who refer to only famous past lives and make general promises. I know of more than a dozen people around the country who were told they were Cleopatra in a past life. After all, I know this can't be true because I was Cleopatra. ☺

A good psychic will be able to pick up on the good and the bad and will be able to help direct you to overcoming the negative in creative and productive ways.

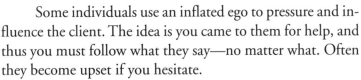

11. Does the psychic demand and expect automatic acceptance?

Some individuals use an inflated ego to pressure and influence the client. The idea is you came to them for help, and thus you must follow what they say—no matter what. Often they become upset if you hesitate.

Usually such arrogance reflects insecurity, but it is manipulative as well. It is a way of saying, "I am the gifted one." It implies that the psychic knows best for you. This is very dangerous, as many people get involved in cults and cult-like activities by giving in to such pressure.

No matter how much a psychic, healer, or teacher demands acceptance, if you are not comfortable with the demand, do not follow it. Honor yourself and what you are feeling. Ultimately, no one knows better for you than you, and a reputable psychic will not try and make you feel pressured in any way.

12.   Is the psychic's own life unhealthy and chaotic?

This is often our first clue to the legitimacy of the psychic. If he or she is extremely unhealthy and their life is chaotic, there is something wrong. Remember that intuition must work through the individual. If the individual leads a life of drugs, alcohol, and other bad health habits, the message is going to come through a little distorted. The message is only as clear as the channel through which it flows.

This does not mean that we must become or seek out ascetic vegetarians who lead a safe, cloistered life. It means that there must be fresh air, a balanced diet, some exercise, and a continuing effort to be productive and growing in life. Physical, emotional, mental, and spiritual health should be striven for. When there is a lack of this, it is usually obvious in the dress and behaviors of the individuals.

DISCERNING FALSE
PSYCHISM AND CHANNELING

1. You are told you may not understand the message, but accept it because it sounds educated.

2. You are told to accept message because the spirit entity is or was a high teacher. (It often cannot be proved.)

3. Psychic or channeler provides no additional teachings, but only reflections of teachings of others or teachings which cannot be verified.

4. Psychic or channeler hides behind material that is vague or gives distant prophecies that pressure your emotions.

5. Psychic or channeler provides material that contradicts itself or previous teachings, including that of recognized masters and teachers.

6. The psychic's or channeler's message has more of an emotional appeal, creating an emotional response, often through fear or flattery.

7. The psychic or channeler displays greater and greater vanity and pride.

8. The psychic or channel develops a spirit of criticism and subtly distorts teachings, often attacking the teachings of others.

9. Psychic or channeler does not live up to standards he or she presents.

10. The psychic's or channeler's mind is gradually becoming scattered, automatic, and lacking in creative expression.

11. Psychic or channeler is experiencing a gradual loss of health and joy, imbued with fear, suspicion and aggressiveness. There is often an accusatory projection toward others with an attitude of, "No one knows better than me."

12. Psychic or channeler has a growing infusion of the idea that everything needed for growth and evolvement can be found within, that nothing is ever needed from outside.

13. Psychic or channeler displays variety of nervous and emotional problems manifesting within three to five years as his or her nervous system starts to degenerate.

14. Psychic or channeler finds it increasingly difficult to hide emotional, physical, financial, or spiritual imbalances.

15. Psychic or channeler experiences poor health and general degeneration on many levels as the entities quit working through the channel and their withdrawal stimulates imbalances.

Chapter 14

Entering the Psychic Realm

A person starts to live
when he can live outside of himself.
Albert Einstein

Today, there are many people striving to develop their sensitivity so they can work professionally as a psychic counselor. There is nothing wrong with this, but there is a great responsibility. Psychic development always increases your sensitivity in all experiences.

The process of becoming is time consuming, and some people do not wish to put forth the time and energy necessary for the true flow of knowledge, understanding and wisdom within their lives. Assimilating true knowledge is what enables us to manifest the more intense spiritual energies of the universe without short circuiting our lives in the process. Failure to prepare appropriately has a similar effect to running high voltage through low voltage wires. They may handle it at first, but eventually there will be a melt down.

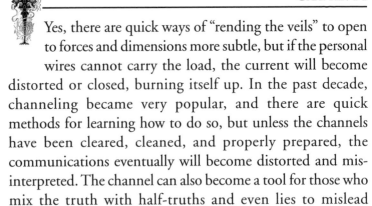

Yes, there are quick ways of "rending the veils" to open to forces and dimensions more subtle, but if the personal wires cannot carry the load, the current will become distorted or closed, burning itself up. In the past decade, channeling became very popular, and there are quick methods for learning how to do so, but unless the channels have been cleared, cleaned, and properly prepared, the communications eventually will become distorted and misinterpreted. The channel can also become a tool for those who mix the truth with half-truths and even lies to mislead individuals. Such beings, physical and non-physical, do exist and so constant vigilance is required.

A Healthy Balance Is Needed

It is dangerous to enter the spiritual, more subtle realms of life and energy with a thinking that has only been strengthened through meditation, gathering information, or mere psychic development. There needs to be an in-depth study and knowledge of the entire path of esoteric schooling in order to truly heal and intensify soul activities and to balance the events of one's life and align it with the universal process.

Frequently those with just a little knowledge feel they are constantly in control when in reality they are not. Unfortunately, the true realization of not being in control does not occur until it is usually too late. Even if techniques have been "learned" in previous lives, which many psychics and modern day pseudo-mystics credit for their facility, it still requires proper training to awaken the potentials in the safest, most beneficial manner.

Most problems arise from dabbling, experimentation, and thrill seeking. Even those who study legitimately to develop their intuitive and psychic abilities will experience phenomena that can be a bit disconcerting. As psychic and creative blockages are removed through proper development practices, poltergeist-type activity often results. The awakening psychic energy can manifest in a variety of phenomena. Isolated noises are heard. Objects move and even phantoms are experienced and a new flow of creative energy is released. As we develop control over our abilities, the inappropriate phenomena disappears.

True psychic ability demands discernment and discrimination involving a way of awakening and integrating our abilities on a soul level. Attainment of psychic power as an end in itself rather than as an aspect of spiritual development is referred to in the East as the *laukika* method of development. In that method, the abilities and powers obtained are only for the present personality, and because true spiritual safeguards are not employed, it is extremely likely that the abilities and powers will be misused.

As long as the we maintain good health, balance, and habits, we will not have ANY major problems when entering the psychic or spiritual realm. By practicing the exercises described in Part II, we can keep our energies at a high and balanced level.

If we are experiencing trauma or depression or become involved in unhealthy activities, we will be more likely to experience some difficulties with inappropriate psychic phenomena. Anytime we begin to recognize imbalances and difficulties, we need to put aside our psychic development efforts until we have regained our sense of a healthy balance.

WAYS TO RECOGNIZE
IMBALANCES AND DIFFICULTIES

1. You find yourself becoming self-centered. Other things and people within your life seem to be increasingly intrusive.

2. You may find yourself motivated more and more by greed, lust, and a desire for knowledge and power.

3. You find yourself wanting to always be out in front of people. This includes wanting to make sure everyone knows how knowledgeable you are. It also includes feelings of knowing better than anyone else.

4. You may find yourself working with speedier and less troublesome methods of developing psychic faculties. This includes focusing solely on psychic phenomena, and even psychic thrill seeking.

5. You may find yourself expressing the new energies and abilities in a misplaced manner such as sexual gratification or power over others. This may even involve ancient, inappropriate methods to attain effects.

6. You may develop premature trance, premature in that you do not have the development of accurate intuition, clairvoyance, and a solid knowledge base to discriminate what and who works through you.

7. You display increasing hypersensitivity in many areas of your life.

Developing Psychic Mediatorship

Positive psychism and intuition requires control of all our senses, with the ability to turn them on and off at will. These abilities should always serve the progress and growth of others and ourselves.

I know many psychics and professionals in this field, and it is amazing how many express difficulty in perceiving and "reading" for themselves. Yes, it is sometimes difficult being objective with ourselves. Often we get caught in the quandary of whether we are perceiving only what we want to see or what actually is. This is called "being human."

We don't want to beat ourselves up over it, but we also must continually work to develop greater and increasingly accurate perceptions in our own lives. The more objective and perceptive we become in our own lives, the better we will be with others. But we have to first be able to apply our skills to our own lives, developing them appropriately.

Our abilities should also always emphasize light and love. As we develop them we must learn to consciously use them at the right time, in the right way, in the right proportion, and for the right person. This is very difficult.

For this reason we should be cautious about working with the public too soon. This dissipates the psychic energy that would otherwise be used to transmute our own energies into a permanent vibration of spirituality. Healing and dream work do this most easily with the least possibility of imbalances. As we learn to heal others, we also balance and heal ourselves.

We should always work to develop psychic or spiritual *mediatorship,* which is the ability to act consciously between a

VARIOUS ASTRAL
AND PSYCHIC PHENOMENA

- mediumship
- apportation
- materialization
- precipitation
- clairvoyance
- clairsentience
- levitation
- spirit lights
- firehandling
- transmutation of metals
- production of fire
- psychic healings
- spirit communication
- slate writing

great source of light, love, and power and those who need it. A good psychic mediator—if working with spirit—always knows with whom he or she is in contact.

A mediator always knows what the nature of the message is, for whom the message is intended, and is also skilled in conveying the information so as not to overly influence or intrude upon another's free will. A psychic mediator is always free to refuse anything that does not feel right. By developing a strong mental and intuition sensitivity, the mediator learns to control extraneous astral interference.

The mediator knows the source of all messages and is capable of putting them into a perspective the individual can relate to. He or she is also able to independently test and verify sources and information because of a strong education in all phases of spiritual development and philosophy (past and present). The mediator also has a strong will and control of physical, emotional, mental, intuition, and spiritual energies.

The psychic mediator may not be perfect in all of these things, but he or she should be working toward mastering them. At this stage of development, the responsibility is great. Because of this, preparation is essential. The following list provides some of the basics necessary for those preparing to enter into this field as professionals.

BASICS FOR ENTERING
THE PSYCHIC FIELD

1. Make sure you get some formal counseling training.

2. Balance work with the spirit with other activities.

3. Limit the number of consultations performed for an individual.

4. Let others decide what is best for them.

5. ALWAYS honor client confidentiality at all times!

6. Let the client know that there is always free will.

7. Continually add to your knowledge base.

1. Make sure you get some formal counseling training.

We may be able to receive intuitive impressions and messages from spirit, but we also must know how to present them so that our client can understand and use the information. A good 75 percent of those who seek out psychics do so because of real problems and do not necessarily need psychic input. Counseling and psychic work should go hand in hand.

Develop some solid counseling techniques. There are a lot of approaches and tools that are effective to use during sessions. If unsure of how to use the techniques, audit some counseling classes at local universities or night schools.

One of the simplest tools is called the *sandwich* technique. Start the session with the positive. If there is a troublesome or negative aspect of the session, deal with it in the middle. Present it also in a manner that reveals possible options and solutions. Discussion of problems should reinforce hope and personal control. The session should always end on the more positive aspects.

2. Balance work with the spirit with other activities.

Contact with non-physical states tends to draw our focus and attention from the world around us. It is easy to become dependent on spirit. We must live our life and remember that spirit is there to help us, not to live our lives for us. Be active within your own life. Have activities, hobbies, and interests aside from psychic work.

3. Limit the number of consultations performed for an individual.

Our clients may become too dependent upon us if we read too frequently for them. We are there to guide and help them become more active and creative within their own lives. For most people, there is seldom enough change in their lives to read for them more than once or maybe twice a year.

4. Let others decide what is best for them.

Interpret and mediate, but do not direct! What we say in a counseling session takes on greater importance when there is that psychic connection. The client is in a receptive and passive position and thus more susceptible to our influence. We should remain detached and avoid, as much as possible, personal preferences, likes and dislikes.

5. ALWAYS honor client confidentiality at all times!

There should always be a strong sense of professionalism about your work. No one but you and the client have the right to know what is said or occurs during a session. If the client wishes to speak of it to others, fine, but as the professional, we do not have that right to share this information— at least not without the client's permission. It is a matter of trust. Unfortunately I have seen many "professionals" discussing and dishing out the gossip acquired during their sessions.

6. Let the client know that there is always free will.

Nothing is ever written in stone, and there is always the possibility of misinterpreting for the client. Most psychic predictions are the result of picking up a pattern, a tendency, or a greater possibility. In general, people rarely change their patterns, so the level of correct predictability can be quite high. The client always has free will, and part of the responsibility of the professional psychic is to help the client see creative possibilities, even within the limitations of what has been occurring in the client's life.

7. Continually add to your knowledge base.

Work to learn more constantly. Read, study, and explore. The more you know, the better you will be at teaching and helping others. Take formal and informal workshops and classes or audit college courses.

Learn and experiment with new techniques. Develop more tools to work with. Strive to add new dimensions to your life and to your work, psychic or otherwise. Every year in the fall I take on something new. Sometimes I take a new class to add a new dimension to something old; other times I try to initiate a new activity into my life. This has helped me to stay creative and productive, keeping me grounded and energized at the same time.

CRYSTALLOMANCY
A form of divination by means of crystal gazing
(Painting by G.P. Jacomb-Hood, modern English artist)

Finding a Spiritual Teacher

A teacher who is working from a true spiritual and soul level can be recognized by a variety of characteristics. First of all, the individual becomes increasingly magnetic, drawing more and more people to him or her. He or she has an ever expanding field of influence and service. At the same time, a true spiritual teacher never professes to know everything, but can direct us to the right book or even another teacher.

The teacher or psychic will demonstrate the virtues of humility, harmlessness, sincerity, and simplicity. He or she will have a strong sense of unity and live to the highest standard in speech and action.

Those who work with true spiritual impressions are highly organized. They have developed their minds, hearts, and intuition. They are creatively productive in many fields and have long years of service to others.

True spiritual teachers are powerhouses of psychic energy which encourages, heals, leads, and protects others. They have increasing control over urges and drives with the power to transmute them into higher expressions. They never make self claims and they do not force their demands on others.

True spiritual teachers increasingly work with the universal laws of privacy and responsibility. Such an individual may be able to know about us, but higher spiritual law does not permit the teacher to interfere with the karma, the learning, of others. As the power of true spiritual expression unfolds, so does the power to influence others, for good or bad.

These individuals may see, but they won't necessarily tell us what they see. They may not try to heal us, but we are touched by healing energies when in their presence. Spiritual teachers do not reveal directly to us, but our higher nature is

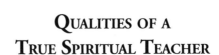

Qualities of a True Spiritual Teacher

1. Always inspires and tries to be of benefit.

2. Energizes and increases creativity, vitality, and joy.

3. Stays open to new teachings, building or continuing earlier wisdom, willing to look at a new angle, approach, greater depth, and synthesis.

4. Deals in wholes and in the interest of humanity.

5. Stimulates need to develop proper expansion of consciousness and service.

6. Evokes mental and intuitive responses.

7. Strengthens our will and enlightens our mind so we can assert ourselves to reach our own goals.

8. Encourages, heals, guides, and protects us.

9. Blesses our life by giving greater meaning to it, inspiring us to reach our own goals.

so stimulated by their presence that we begin to see and understand things never before seen or understood.

Contact with true spiritual teachers is a blessing we feel. It strengthens our will and enlightens our mind so we can exert ourselves to reach our own goals. We experience a greater ability to touch others within our own life as well.

The true spiritual teacher gives greater meaning to life by demonstrating a sense of duty and sacrificial acts in relationships. Theirs is a conscious and intuitive ability to know karma and to cooperate with its laws in regard to themselves and to all those they touch.

Knowledge Is Power

There is an old saying "knowledge is power" and this is doubly true as we open more and more to the psychic and spiritual realms. For each of us, the question of how we will use our gifts in an ethical manner is one that will require deep introspection and a personal examination of our values and our intentions.

As psychics, we hold a great deal of power to influence other people, rightly or wrongly. People will tend to give more significance to what we say because of the magic associated with the psychic realm. Therefore it is critical to be clear about our intentions, motives, and objectives when providing others with information. The following goals or objectives should be carefully considered:

- helping the client gain greater insight or objectivity about his or her situation

- helping the client to understand his or her role in the situation, as well as, how his or her actions may be affecting the situation—positively and negatively

- helping the client to understand his or her responsibilities regarding the situation

- helping the client to discover new solutions to situation

- helping the client to better understand his or her patterns of relating to others

- providing the client with personal information about his or her motives

- educating others about the value of psychic development as a tool for inner growth and awareness

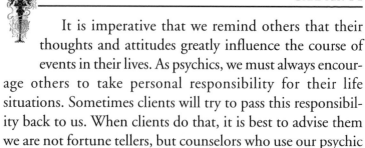

It is imperative that we remind others that their thoughts and attitudes greatly influence the course of events in their lives. As psychics, we must always encourage others to take personal responsibility for their life situations. Sometimes clients will try to pass this responsibility back to us. When clients do that, it is best to advise them we are not fortune tellers, but counselors who use our psychic gifts as a tool to help others.

Because psychic readings are so often associated with fortune telling by the general public, it is helpful before the appointment to tell clients about your philosophy and the method you will use during the reading. On the following page, I've listed a number of items that I use when describing my philosophy. Over the years, my philosophy has evolved into a personal code of ethics that I maintain in my relationships with others.

Of course, The Golden Rule is also a good standard to use when working with others. Simply by "doing unto others as you would have them do unto you" can help avoid compromising your values when dealing with others. Over time, you will learn to trust yourself more and more and you won't be afraid to say "No" to a client's request for confidential information that involves invading the privacy of other individuals.

Always remember, as a psychic, you are one of the keepers of the keys to the psychic kingdom. Go forth and use your gifts wisely!

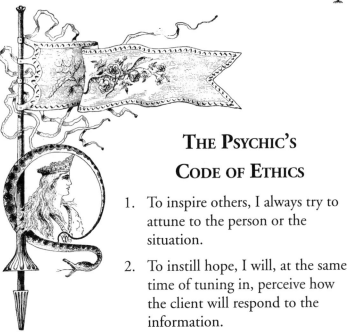

THE PSYCHIC'S
CODE OF ETHICS

1. To inspire others, I always try to attune to the person or the situation.

2. To instill hope, I will, at the same time of tuning in, perceive how the client will respond to the information.

3. To educate, I will express my insights in a non-threatening manner, passing helpful information along in a loving, productive, and positive way so it can be better received by the client.

4. To increase faith, I will always express the information in a manner that will be understood by the client.

5. To be of service, I will rely on my insight to identify new possibilities and beneficial options or courses of action to the client's situation.

6. To build trust, I will do all of the above without intruding upon the free will of the client.

Appendix A

Exercise and Tool Quick Reference

benefits and desired results of the exercises and tools arranged alphabetically

EXERCISES

Desired Results	Exercises
ACTIVATE CREATIVITY	Making Your Sacred Power Shield
ALIGHMENT WITH DIVINE FORCES	Awakening Ancient Divine Forces
ANGELIC PROTECTION	Angelic Talisman
ASSERTIVENESS WITH PROBLEMS	Aligning with Our Predator Guardians
ATTUNE TO NATURE	Adopting the Adaptive Behavior of Animal Guardians, Aligning with Our Predator Guardians, Sacred Walk
AWAKEN HOPE	Angelic Talisman
BALANCE	Ida-Pingala Exercise Making Your Sacred Power Shield Middle Pillar of Light Posture of Protection Qabalistic Cross Roses of Light
BLESS	Sacred Walk
CALM	Angelic Talisman Middle Pillar of Light Posture of Protection Qabalistic Cross Sacred Walk
CLEANSE	Banishing Ritual of the Pentagram Cleansing White Fire Vortex

AND TOOLS

Colored Candles	Aroma-therapy	Flower Elixirs	Trees
colors of the tradition			hawthorn, peach
colors of the tradition			
colors of the tradition			
			elm, hawthorn
silver, white, colors of the tradition	cedar	pine, rose	cherry
rainbow hues, colors of the tradition (Power Shield)	Rescue Remedy		orange
	carnation, rose		
colors of the tradition (Angelic Talisman)	cedar, eucalyptus	pine, Rescue Remedy, white chestnut, yarrow	aspen, peach, pine
white	cedar, lemon, sage	crab apple, pennyroyal, pine, sage	eucalyptus, lemon

Ted Andrews

EXERCISES

Desired Results	Exercises
CONTROL OVER ENERGIES	Aligning with Our Predator Guardians
DISCONNECT FROM EMPATHIC RESPONSES	Cleansing White Fire Vortex
GAIN INSIGHT	Angelic Talisman Roses of Light Sacred Walk
GROUNDING	Banishing Ritual of the Pentagram Cleansing White Fire Vortex Posture of Protection Sacred Walk
HANDLING OPPOSITION	Adopting the Adaptive Behavior of Animal Guardians
HEAL	Ida-Pingala Exercise Making Your Sacred Power Shield Middle Pillar of Light Roses of Light Sacred Walk
INCREASE ENERGY AND VITALITY	Ida-Pingala Exercise Middle Piller of Light
PREPARE FOR PSYCHIC WORK	Cleansing White Fire Vortex
PREVENT ENERGY DRAINS	Posture of Protection
PROTECTION	Aligning with Our Predator Guardians Angelic Talisman Awakening Ancient Divine Forces Making Your Sacred Power Shield

AND TOOLS

Colored Candles	Aroma-therapy	Flower Elixirs	Trees
	eucalyptus		
brown	gardenia		fig
black, silver, white, colors of the tradition (Angelic Talisman)	frankincense, lemon	shasta daisy, walnut, yarrow	honeysuckle
black, brown	sage		maple
rainbow hues, white, colors of the tradition (Power Shield)	carnation	sage	apple, birch, cedar, cypress, elder eucalyptus, willow
		olive	
		lavender	
	gardenia		
black, colors of the tradition	cedar frankincense	lavender, pennyroyal	cedar, elder, holly, lemon, palm

EXERCISES

Desired Results	Exercises
PURIFYING	Banishing Ritual of the Pentagram Cleansing White Fire Vortex
RELIEVE STRESS AND WORRY	Sacred Walk
REPEL NEGATIVITY	Banishing Ritual of the Pentagram Posture of Protection
RESOLVE PROBLEMS	Aligning with Our Predator Guardians
RESTORE LOST ENERGY	Ida-Pingala Exercise
SHARPEN SENSES IN CASE OF PSYCHIC ATTACKS	Banishing Ritual of the Pentagram Aligning with Our Predator Guardians
SPIRITUAL GUIDANCE	Awakening Ancient Divine Forces
STABILIZING	Qabalistic Cross Sacred Walk
STRENGTHEN AURA	Angelilc Talisman Making Your Power Shield Middle Pillar of Light Posture of Protection Roses of Light Sacred Walk
STRENGTHEN FOCUS	Qabalistic Cross

AND TOOLS

Colored Candles	Aroma-therapy	Flower Elixirs	Trees
			lemon
	lemon, sage	Rescue Remedy, yarrow	elm
		shasta daisy, white chestnut	palm
brown, silver			
colors of the tradition			
black, brown		Rescue Remedy	
black, colors of the tradition (Power Shield)	carnation, gardenia	oak, sage, walnut, yarrow	oak

Andrews, Ted. *Animal-Speak*. St. Paul, MN: Llewellyn Publications, 1993.

_____. *Crystal Balls and Crystal Bowls*. St. Paul, MN: Llewellyn Publications, 1994.

_____. *Dream Alchemy*. St. Paul, MN: Llewellyn Publications, 1991.

_____. *Enchantment of the Faerie Realm*. St. Paul, MN: Llewellyn Publications, 1992.

_____. *The Healer's Manual*. St. Paul, MN: Llewellyn Publications, 1993.

_____. *How to Heal with Color*. St. Paul, MN: Llewellyn Publications, 1992.

_____. *How to Develop and Use Psychic Touch*. St. Paul, MN: Llewellyn Publications, 1994.

_____. *How to Meet and Work with Spirit Guides*. St. Paul, MN: Llewellyn Publications, 1992.

_____. *How to See and Read the Aura*. St. Paul, MN: Llewellyn Publications, 1991.

_____. *How to Uncover Your Past Lives*. St. Paul, MN: Llewellyn Publications, 1992.

_____. *Magickal Dance*. St. Paul, MN: Llewellyn Publications, 1992.

_____. *More Simplified Magic*. Jackson, TN: Dragonhawk Publishing, 1998.

_____. *Music Theraphy for Non-Musicians*. Batavia, OH: Dragonhawk Publishing, 1997.

_____. *Sacred Sounds*. St. Paul, MN: Llewellyn Publications, 1992.

_____. *Simplified Magic*. St. Paul, MN: Llewellyn Publications, 1989.

_____. *The Magical Name*. St. Paul, MN: Llewellyn Publications, 1990

_____. *The Occult Christ: Angelic Mysteries and the Divine Feminine*. St. Paul, MN: Llewellyn Publications, 1993.

_____. *Treasures of the Unicorn*. Batavia, OH: Dragonhawk Publishing, 1996.

Becker, Robert and Seldon, Gary. *The Body Electric*. New York, NY: William Morrow, 1985.

Brennon, J.H. *Astral Doorways*. Northamptonshire, GB: Aquarian Press, 1986.

Buckland, Raymond. *Practical Candleburning Rituals*. St. Paul, MN: Llewellyn Publications, 1982.

Cooper, J.C. *Symbolism: The Universal Language.* Northamptonshire, GB: Aquarian Press, 1982.

Cunningham, Scott. *Cunningham's Encyclopedia of Magickal Herbs.* St. Paul, MN: Llewellyn Publications, 1985.

Fettner, Ann Tucker. *Potpouri, Incense and Fragrant Concoctions.* New York, NY: Workman Publishing, 1977.

Gawain, Shakti. *Creative Visualization.* Mill Valley,CA: Whatever Publishing, 1978.

Davidson, Gustav. *Dictionary of Angels.* Free Press; 1967.

Denning, Melita and Phillips, Osborne. *Psychic Self-Defense and Well-Being.* St. Paul, MN: Llewellyn Publications,1985.

Fortune, Dion. *Aspects of Occultism.* Northamptonshire, GB: Aquarian Press, 1986.

_____. *Practical Occultism in Daily Life.* Northamptonshire, GB: Aquarian Press, 1981.

_____. *Psychic Self-Defense.* Northamptonshire, GB: Aquarian Press, 1984.

Hall, Manly P. *Man: Grand Symbol of the Mysteries.* Los Angeles, CA: Philosophical Research Society, 1972.

_____.*Secret Teachings of the Ages.* Los Angeles, CA: Philosophical Research Society, 1977.

Jung, Carl. *Archetypes and the Collective Unconscious* in *The Collected Works of C.J. Jung.* Vol. 18. Princeton, NJ: Princeton University Press, 1976.

Miller, Richard Allen. *Magickal and Ritual Use of Herbs.* Destiny Books, 1983.

Richardson, Alan. *Gift of the Moon.* Northamptonshire, GB: Aquarian Press, 1984.

Schure, Edouard. *From the Sphinx to the Christ.* San Francisco, CA: Harper and Row, 1970.

Steiner, Rudolph. *An Outline of Occult Science.* Hudson, NY: Anthroposiphical Press, 1972.

_____. *Knowledge of the Higher Worlds.* Hudson, NY: Anthroposiphical Press, 1947.

_____. *Spiritual Hierarchies.* Hudson, NY: Anthroposiphical Press, 1970.

Weinstein, Marion. *Positive Magic.* Boulder CO: Phoenix Publishing, 1978.

ROSES OF LIGHT

45 minutes
Retail: $10

SEE PAGES
192-196

Available
through all
major
distributors and
all major
bookstores

Roses of Light

HEALING

HARMONIES

Ted Andrews

At the heart of all the ancient traditions was the teaching of sound, music, and voice to help heal, enlighten, and awaken higher consciousness. Roses of Light is an audio cassette of healing harmonies to relax and balance the body, mind, and spirit. It will strengthen the aura and align the chakras. It will renew health and joy.

Music and words composed and performed by Ted Andrews

SIDE 1: ROSES OF LIGHT (HEALING MUSIC)
SIDE 2: ROSES OF LIGHT
(GUIDED MEDITATION AND HEALING MUSIC)

ISBN 1-888767-00-6

PSYCHIC PROTECTION

50 minutes
Retail: $10

Available through all major distributors and all major bookstores

From the best selling books:
HOW TO SEE AND READ THE AURA
SIMPLIFIED MAGIC

SEE PAGES
143-150,
266-275

This cassette provides two of the most powerful and beneficial exercises for overall balance, health, and protection. It is essential for anyone working within the psychic field or developing his or her own psychic abilities. Recommended for those in healing or social work, and encouraged for the well-being of the average individual.

The key to protecting ourselves is the aura, the energy field surrounding the human body. These exercises will strengthen and purify the aura and our environment.

Music and words composed and performed by Ted Andrews

SIDE 1: THE MIDDLE PILLAR EXERCISE

SIDE 2: THE BANISHING RITUAL OF THE PENTAGRAM
(INCLUDES THE QABALISTIC CROSS)

ISBN 1-888767-04-9

ABOUT THE AUTHOR

Ted Andrews

Ted Andrews is an internationally recognized author, storyteller, teacher, and mystic. A leader in the human potential and metaphysical fields, his books have been translated into fifteen foreign languages, and he is often featured on such national and local television and radio networks such as CBS, NBC, FOX, CNBC, and others.

A teacher and counsellor in the public school system for ten years, Ted has an extensive formal and informal education. He has been involved in the study of esoteric, the occult, and holistic health for over 30 years and is known for his dynamic and practical seminars and his ability to make the mystical accessible to everyone.

Called a true Renaissance man, Ted is schooled in music and has composed, performed, and produced the music for ten audio cassettes. He has worked as a holistic healer, with a focus upon creating individualized musical therapies, and Ted is also a continuing student of the ballet and Kung Fu. He holds state and federal permits to work with his own birds of prey, and conducts animal education and story-telling programs throughout the United States.

TO WRITE TO THE AUTHOR

Ted appreciates hearing from readers, learning of their enjoyment and benefits of his books. Letters to the author may be sent to the following address:

Ted Andrews
c/o Dragonhawk Publishing
P.O. Box 1316
Jackson, Tennessee   38302-1316